Christina Rossetti

CHRISTINA ROSSETTI

Colored chalk portrait of Christina Rossetti by Dante Gabriel Rossetti, 1866.

Christina Rossetti

Critical Perspectives, 1862–1982

Edna Kotin Charles

Selinsgrove: Susquehanna University Press
London and Toronto: Associated University Presses

Associated University Presses
440 Forsgate Drive
Cranbury, NJ 08512

Associated University Presses
25 Sicilian Avenue
London WC1A 2QH, England

Associated University Presses
2133 Royal Windsor Drive
Unit 1
Mississauga, Ontario
Canada L5J 1K5

Library of Congress Cataloging in Publication Data

Charles, Edna Kotin, 1921–
  Christina Rossetti, critical perspectives, 1862–1982.

  Bibliography: p.
  Includes index.
  1. Rossetti, Christina Georgina, 1830–1894—Criticism and interpretation—
History. —. Title.
PR5238.C48 1985   821'.8   84-40392
ISBN 0-941664-06-6

Printed in the United States of America

For Saul,
May, Eva, Linda, Amy, Robert, Marc, Amy Lynn,
Craig, Jessica, Andrew,
and to the memory of my father
Charles Kotin

Contents

Illustrations

Acknowledgments

It is with great pleasure that I offer here, in acknowledgment of their help, a slight token of my gratitude for the consistent support and helpful suggestions given me by my colleagues at Fairleigh Dickinson University: Professors Lois Gordon, Vernon Schonert, John Becker, and Vartkis Kinoian.

Librarians at the Weiner Library of Fairleigh Dickinson University deserve both my appreciation and respect. Among those to whom I owe particular thanks are Ruth Schwartz, Director of Libraries, Mary McMahon, and Laila Rogers, for their amazing ability to trace obscure sources and to find elusive library materials necessary to the project. My gratitude as well to Susan Woolfson who carefully pondered my manuscript and provided excellent editorial advice and to Katherine Balik for her unfailing patience and efficient secretarial skills.

I acknowledge with affection and gratitude my deep indebtedness to Nasrollah S. Fatemi, Distinguished Professor Emeritus of International Affairs and Consultant of the Institute of Graduate International Studies at Fairleigh Dickinson University, for his unfailing encouragement and valuable assistance.

Finally, to my husband, Saul Charles, I owe the most important debt: a belief in the necessity of my commitment to scholarship and a conviction that my work was valuable.

Introduction

The Victorian century claimed Christina Rossetti as its own, but her poetry has commanded the attention of critics in the twentieth. And today there is heightened interest in the works of the woman who, new critical perspectives reveal, may well have conducted a fierce inner struggle against assuming the role of a middle-class Victorian woman. Certainly it is time for an extensive review of the critical reception Christina Rossetti's poems have received in Britain and the United States since the publication of her first volume in 1862.

This volume undertakes just such a review of the entire body of scholarship and criticism—from book chapters to book-length studies, from magazine articles to doctoral dissertations—relating to Rossetti's poetic endeavors.[1] It is divided into three sections— the first devoted to the years 1862–99, in which the poet's work was judged by her contemporaries; the second to the years 1900– 1939—the start of a new century and in many discernible ways a transitional period for the critical enterprise; and the third to the years 1940–82, which have seen the flowering of the Freudian and Jungian approaches to literature and the steady growth of a feminist one.

More than a bibliographical guide to criticism and scholarship, the present volume both summarizes and explains the changing interests evinced by critics of Rossetti's works during these three periods and up to the present year. The weight given in each era to such matters as biography, figurative language, theme, supernaturalism, metrics, diction, as well as to particular poems comes under scrutiny. In each category, there are representative samples of the variety of judgments offered. As an aid to comprehension and comprehensiveness, there are pertinent excerpts from Rossetti's poetry itself.

For the researcher into particular aspects of Christina Rossetti's poetry, this work of summarization and categorization will shed light on the poet and her era. It may also facilitate comparisons of the critical enterprise in the several periods covered and of the critical reception given other poets of the Victorian era.

This endeavor anticipates the publication of not one but two complete editions of the Rossetti opus[2]—a happy if belated event these fifty years after the poet's centennial.

Christina Rossetti wrote over nine hundred poems in English and sixty in Italian, the majority of them devotional or religious in subject and mood. In 1847, her grandfather Gaetano Polidori printed *Verses*, a small volume of her poetry, on his private press. In 1862, Christina issued *Goblin Market and Other Poems*, a volume containing many of the poems she had written since 1848. The title poem, "Goblin Market," remains her most famous single poem, though the volume also included some regarded as her best. The popularity of the first volume encouraged Rossetti to produce still other books of poetry: The *Prince's Progress and Other Poems* (1866); *Sing-Song* (1872); and *A Pageant and Other Poems* (1881), which included the well-known *Monna Innominata* sonnet sequence. *Verses* (1893) and *New Poems* (1896) were published posthumously. She also wrote a mixture of poetry and prose—*Called to Be Saints* (1881); *Time Flies* (1885); and *The Face of the Deep* (1892)—and issued several purely prose works—*Commonplace and Other Short Stories* (1870); *Annus Domini* (1874); *Speaking Likenesses* (1874); and *Seek and Find* (1879). *Maude*, printed posthumously, was written in 1850.

Christina Rossetti was twenty when she offered her poems for formal publication. These early poems were submitted to the Pre-Raphaelite journal, *The Germ*, where, in 1850 they began appearing anonymously or under the name Ellen Alleyn. The pseudonym was suggested by her brother Dante Gabriel Rossetti, a founder of the Pre-Raphaelite movement—the brotherhood of painters and poets who, seeking refuge from the materialism of industrialized England, attempted to recapture the beauty, spirituality, and comparative simplicity of the medieval world.

With the publication of *Goblin Market and Other Poems* in 1862, Christina was accorded a degree of fame in literary circles that were encouraging the work of the Pre-Raphaelites. The title poem received wide general notice—its unique and fantastic elements were commented on at length—but mixed reviews, although for the volume's devotional poems there was almost unanimous praise. Inevitably, Christina's work was compared with that of Dante Gabriel, whose talent was seen to overshadow hers.

The Prince's Progress and Other Poems of 1866 was less well received, but its publication brought recognition of Christina Rossetti as a rising minor female poet, and a new comparison—this time with another "recognized minor female poet," Jean Ingelow. Beside *her* work, Rossetti's was said to pale somewhat.

A book of children's verses, *Sing-Song*, published in 1870, was widely admired, but it was not until 1881, with the publication of *A Pageant and Other Poems*, containing the *Monna Innominata* sonnets, that Rossetti gained her greatest acclaim. It was then that critics of note sought to compare Rossetti's work with that of the female poet *par excellence*, Elizabeth Barrett Browning, in *Sonnets from the Portuguese*—though few ceded first place to Rossetti.

With Christina Rossetti's death in 1894 came an outpouring of praise by reviewers and friends of the Rossetti family that reached eulogistic heights. Among the contributors to England's religious and conservative presses there was praise for Rossetti's melodious voice, her love of nature and of all growing things, her compassion for the smallest of creatures. Now she was proclaimed a greater poet than Felicia Hemans, Dora Greenwell, and Adelaide Proctor—nineteenth-century women whose verses had gained a limited popularity during the Victorian age but would fade from notice in the first few decades of the new century—and vied for critical popularity with Jean Ingelow and Mrs. Browning. None in this group, however, was seen to inhabit the same stratum as any male poet of the age.

In the early twentieth century, Rossetti's star shone more brightly than Mrs. Browning's, for reasons that appear at once aesthetic and social. Elisabeth Luther Cary suggests in her 1900 biography of Rossetti that earlier critics preferred Mrs. Browning's sonnets to Christina Rossetti's because the former's overflowed with the happiness of fulfilled love, while the latter's expressed frustrated, unrealized love. In the new century, however, it was to the qualities of simplicity, technical excellence, and spiritual beauty in Rossetti's work that the critics directed their attention; her verses then recommended themselves over the eloquent but sometimes oversentimentalized and blurring passages of "the happier lover and lesser poet."[3]

Critics did acknowledge Mrs. Browning as the more intellectual poet of the two and saw her subject matter as wider in scope than Christina Rossetti's—a factor that has figured in judgments of

Rossetti's corpus in more recent years. But at the same time, Browning was rebuked, most often by male critics, for her display of scholarship and address of political topics—the preserve, traditionally, of males—and Rossetti praised in turn for her "maiden delicacy" and passivity. Critics were, however, willing to place Rossetti in the company of the great, male religious voices of the seventeenth century—Donne, Herbert, Vaughan, Crashaw, Herrick—and even alongside one Victorian, Cardinal Newman. Several went so far as to acclaim her the greatest religious voice of all time.

At the centenary of Rossetti's birth in 1930, and for half a decade thereafter, there was again an outpouring of tributes in both English and American periodicals, and in chapters and full-length studies published by trade and university presses. There was a brief abatement, and then, in the 1940s, came yet another surge of interest in Rossetti's works, this time by those wielding the tools of Freudian and Jungian analysis. This last enterprise continues through the present and has been taken up most recently by critics who fall under the rubric "feminist."

Today, Rossetti's poetry is more widely read and of keener interest to critics than ever before, and not only in the English-speaking world but on the Continent as well. An index of her popularity can be seen in the several new editions of selected poetry, in biographical-critical studies, doctoral dissertations, and articles in literary periodicals of distinction. Anthologies of Victorian writings typically include selections from the whole range of Rossetti's works—long narrative poems, the ghost poems, nature poems, children's verses, and devotional pieces. Although still rated below the acknowledged "big three" of the Victorian Age—Alfred, Lord Tennyson, Robert Browning, and Matthew Arnold—she is no longer the novice, the "minor female poet" and younger sister of Dante Gabriel Rossetti, but in the company of other Victorian poets of stature—George Meredith, Gerard Manley Hopkins, William Morris, Algernon Charles Swinburne, Thomas Hardy, A. E. Housman, and Dante Gabriel himself.

One of Christina Rossetti's favorite poets was John Keats. It was her brother who had introduced her to his works as well as to those of Shakespeare, Blake, Crabbe, Coleridge, Shelley, Tennyson, and Robert Browning. Dante Gabriel served as his sister's tutor in many other ways as well, encouraging her to write, offering criticism and counsel, and providing the opportunity for association with such leading figures of the Pre-Raphaelite movement as his friends Holman Hunt and John Millais.

In later years, prominent literary friends of Dante Rossetti were to honor the poet's connection with the brotherhood, Sir Edmund Gosse calling her the "High Priestess of Pre-Raphaelitism," and Swinburne hailing her as the "Jael who led their host [the Pre-Raphaelites] to victory."

Some artists in the group used Christina as a model for their paintings; they seemed to find in her delicate features and lustrous hair the Pre-Raphaelite ideal of feminine beauty. Indeed, those familiar with Dante Gabriel's *The Girlhood of Mary Virgin* and *Ecce Ancilli Domini* will recognize his sister as the model for Mary. The same love of vivid coloring, the details of jewels, flowers, fruits, tapestries, and fascination with the supernatural are richly on display in Christina Rossetti's works as well.

One also sees the effect in the poet's work of her involvement with the Oxford Movement of the High Anglican Church, which opposed both the liberal tendencies in the English church and Romanism's Mariolatry and supplication of the saints. The work of John Keble, the austere poetic voice of the Oxford Movement, was particularly appealing to Christina Rossetti, as were the stirring sermons of the Reverend William Dodsworth, whose services at Christ Church were attended by the Rossetti family. And the Movement's effect was not only on her poetry. By her unprententious, retiring existence, Rossetti was living its teachings as well. In matters of faith and piety, it appears to have been Mrs. Rossetti who led the way for her daughter.

One detects too a Romantic strain in Christina Rossetti's works, though Romanticism's strength was considerably dissipated by the second half of the nineteenth century—in her unbounded joy in nature, her evocation of dreary vistas and unearthly landscapes, spectral lovers, and death-doomed heroines. The source, it is speculated, was the English Romantic poetry and novels Christina read in abundance in adolescence.

Other critics and biographers have found echoes of still other early readings in her works. The Rossetti children, educated at home by their mother, were read to from the Bible, St. Augustine, and *Pilgrim's Progress* and made familiar with the Gothic romances of Sir Walter Scott, Ann Radcliffe, Monk Lewis, and Charles Robert Maturin, not to mention the *Arabian Nights*, ostensibly Christina's favorite. Then there is the judgment of biographer

Watercolor portrait of Christina as a child of seven by Filippo Pistrucci, 1837.

Mackenzie Bell, that one cannot "accentuate overmuch" the influence on the poet of her Latin lineage, her early environment, and her introduction, when but a young child, to the Italian classics, and particularly the works of Metastasio, Tasso, and Ariosto.[4]

The poet's life story has thus offered some of the rich ground for speculation about the wellsprings and essential thrust of the works—and is, if anything, being mined with increasing diligence today. Briefly stated:

Christina Rossetti's father, Gabriele, a political refugee from Italy, had married, in London, Frances Polidori, a woman of mixed English and Italian blood but a staunch Anglican. From this union there were four offspring: Maria, born in 1827; Dante Gabriel in 1828; William Michael in 1829; and Christina Georgina in 1830.

In 1852, as the elder Rossetti's health began to fail, he gave up tutoring private pupils in Italian and eventually resigned his post as professor of Italian at Kings College, Oxford. To supplement the family income, Mrs. Rossetti gave French and Italian lessons outside the home; Maria became a resident governess; and William Michael began clerking at the Inland Revenue office in Somerset. Dante Gabriel continued with his art lessons. Christina, the youngest, was expected to take up governess duties when she too came of age, but early in adolescence she became mysteriously ill and melancholy, an illness later diagnosed by her physician as anemia. Later, Mrs. Rossetti made two attempts to run a day school—one in London and another, assisted by Christina, in Frome—but both failed. William Rossetti, at twenty-four, after being promoted at Somerset House, acquired a more comfortable home and invited the Rossetti family to live with him. But soon after the move, Professor Rossetti became critically ill and, in 1854, he died.

At eighteen Christinia was betrothed to James Collinson, an artist friend of her brother's—"in person small and rather dumpy, with a thick neck; his face intelligent maybe but in no wise handsome," according to her brother William.[5] Born an Anglican, he had converted to Catholicism, but to induce Christina to become his wife returned to his original confession. Two years later he returned to the Church of Rome and Christina broke their engagement. William later contended that Collinson "had none the less struck a staggering blow at Christina's peace of mind on the very threshold of womanly life, and a blow from which she did not fully recover."[6]

Frances M. L. Rossetti (Polidori) by Dante Gabriel Rossetti, 1854.

In her early thirties Christina received another proposal of marriage, from Charles Bagot Cayley, a Greek scholar and linguist who had been a student of her father's. Although Cayley was born into the Church of England, his views were unorthodox and the couple's differences in matters of religion are said to have caused Christina to reject his marriage offer, although they remained close friends until his death.

A recent biographer of Christina Rossetti claims it was neither Collinson nor Cayley, but the poet-painter William Bell Scott, who captured her deepest feelings. Scott, a friend of Dante Gabriel and already married when Christina met him at seventeen, was, according to Lona Mosk Packer's hypothesis, the cause of Christina's sense of guilt, horror, and renunciation of human love that is so often given expression in her poetry. Although several critics reviewing her theory acclaim Packer's discoveries for the added insights they provide into Rossetti's poetry, there are many who rebut her "data." William E. Fredeman, for example, in commenting on Packer's work, states: "Circumstantial evidence derived primarily from the poetry makes impossible the precise documentation of a theory for which there is not a single scrap of positive and direct proof."[7]

Christina rarely left London except, when she was very young, for excursions into the countryside, most often to her grandfather Polidori's country cottage in Regent's Park. She was active throughout the 1860s, however, as a volunteer social worker at the St. Mary Magdalene Home for Fallen Women. In her thirties she made two trips to the Continent—a journey to Normandy in 1861 and one to Switzerland and Italy in 1865. In 1871, the poet was afflicted with Graves disease, a thryoid condition which stole her beauty and sapped her strength. Maria, who had entered the All Saints Sisterhood, an Anglican order, in 1872, died in 1876. Cayley died at the age of sixty in 1882; Mrs. Rossetti in 1886; and soon thereafter the two maternal aunts whom Christina had tended devotedly. After 1890 the poet lived as a recluse and died, after a two-year bout with cancer, on December 29, 1894.

Christina Rossetti

Gabriele Rossetti by Dante Gabriel Rossetti, 1853.

1

The Poet-Saint: Criticism, 1862–1899

Every great composition in the world, every great piece of
painting or literature—without any exception, from the birth
of Man to this hour—is an assertion of moral law.

John Ruskin, *Fors Clavigera*

In an age when poetry itself has been pressed into the service of
doubt and denial [Christina Rossetti's] is a message to which
both mind and heart will be vastly the better for listening.

A. Smellie, "Christina Rossetti and Her Message"

By the window was a high narrow reading-desk at which stood
writing a slight girl with a serious regular profile, dark against
the pallid wintry light without. This most interesting to me of
the two inmates turned on my entrance, made the most formal
and graceful courtsey, and resumed her writing, and the old
gentleman, [Rossetti père] signed to a chair for my sitting
down. . . . The girl was Christina, who had already at seventeen written, like her brother, some admirable lyrics, nearly all
overshaded with melancholy. Melancholy I call it, but perhaps
the right word would be pious sentiment. At least in her mind
piety and sadness went together, and have done so all her life.

William Bell Scott, *Autobiographical Notes*

*T*hose who have examined the Victorian frame of mind speak of
the nineteenth-century public's need for a "spiritual absolute" in a
period marked by challenges to traditional beliefs and accepted
forms of progress. In *Fors Clavigera* (1877), as quoted above, the
major arbiter of art and taste, John Ruskin, was holding firm to a

23

timeless standard for judging works of art. Similarly, an intention to hold firm to the conventions of conduct and belief is evident in Smellie's appreciation, in 1895, of Christina Rossetti's works themselves.

Little wonder that he and other critics of the period, in both the secular and religious press, gave the greatest share of critical attention to the poet's "devotional poems"—"The Heart Knoweth Its Own Bitterness," "Old and New Year Ditties," "A Better Resurrection," "Advent," "The Three Enemies," "The World," "A Song for the Least of All Saints," and "The Lowest Place"—and to several of Rossetti's general poems of similar spiritual content, including "Convent Threshold," "Up-hill," "Amor Mundi"—in the course of 160 reviews of Christina Rossetti's works during the years 1862 to 1899 of the Victorian era. These reviews take the form of reminiscences, memorials, sketches, essays, articles, and one book-length study and are almost exclusively by English critics.

Singled out for commendation by approximately a third of the critics is "The Three Enemies" (1851), one of Rossetti's most popular devotional pieces. Typical of their response is that of an anonymous critic for the October 1876, issue of the *Catholic World,* a monthly edited for a lay and clerical audience: "What in the wide realm of English poetry is more beautiful than this?"[1]

The Flesh
'Sweet, thou art pale.'
　　　　　'More pale to see,
Christ hung upon the cruel tree
And bore His Father's wrath for me.' . . .

The World
'Sweet, thou art young.'
　　　　　'So He was young
Who for my sake in silence hung
Upon the Cross with Passion wrung.'

The Devil
'Thou shalt have Knowledge.'
　　　　　'Helpless dust!
In thee, O lord, I put my trust:
Answer Thou for me, Wise and Just.'
'And Might.'—
　　　　　'Get thee behind me. Lord,

Who hast redeemed and not abhorred,
My soul, oh keep it by Thy Word."[2]

The Catholic critic adds a proselytizing note. How much greater
would be the poet's spiritual fulfillment—and how much more
fulfilled her talent—were she a communicant of the Roman
church. Surely a heart like Rossetti's that can express such religious
feelings

> should be safely housed in the one true fold, and there only, can such
> hearts find room for expansion; for there alone can they find the food
> to fill them, the wherewith to satisfy their long yearnings, the light to
> guide the many wanderings of their spirits, the strength to lift up and
> sustain them after many a cruel deceit. Outside that threshold, how-
> ever near they may be to it, they will find their lives empty.[3]

For an anonymous reviewer for the January 16, 1895, issue of the
Dial, a secular weekly of literature, philosophy, and religion, the
final measure of such expressions of religious sentiment is whether
they contain even a hint of "affection, artificiality, or insincerity."
The reviewer sees "no touch" of these in Rossetti's verses. Her
works, he contends, are "unsurpassed and perhaps unequalled by
any of her contemporaries," and he predicts that "Old and New
Year Ditties" (1860) "will long be treasured among the religious
classics of the English language."[4] The poem, written in Rossetti's
thirtieth year, is a solemn acknowledgment of the passing of the
poet's beauty and youth. The third section of this poem is the one
the *Dial* commends, as do most of its critics:

> Passing away, saith the World, passing away:
> Chances, beauty, and youth, sapped day by day:
> Thy life never continueth in one stay.
> Is the eye waxen dim, is the dark hair changing to grey
> That hath won neither laurel nor bay?
> I shall clothe myself in Spring and bud in May:
> Thou, root-stricken, shalt not rebuild thy decay
> On my bosom for aye
> Then I answered: Yea.
>
> Passing away, saith my Soul, passing away:
> With its burden of fear and hope, of labour and play,
> Hearken what the past doth witness and say:
> Rust in thy gold, a moth is in thine array,
> A canker is in thy bud, thy leaf must decay.

At midnight, at cockcrow, at morning, one certain day
Lo the Bridegroom shall come and shall not delay;
Watch thou and pray.
Then I answered: Yea.

Passing away, saith my God, passing away;
Winter passeth after the long delay:
New grapes on the vine, new figs on the tender spray,
Turtle called turtle in Heaven's May.
Though I tarry, wait for Me, trust Me, watch and pray:
Arise, come away, night is past and lo it is day,
My love, My sister, My spouse, thou shalt hear Me say.
Then I answered: Yea.

[191]

The literary critic Edmund K. Chambers, writing in the February 1894, the *Academy,* a weekly review of literature, science, and art, finds the "low-toned" quality of Rossetti's devotional works their most significant feature. The poet has experienced the bitterness and disappointments of life, has seen that all is vanity, and yet "through all she retains a moderate optimism; she is content to walk dimly to hold a humble faith, . . . that man will have a chance of fulfilling his high destinies, and that Love will still be lord of all." This "philosophy of resignation . . . of acceptance,"[5] he says, is well demonstrated in "Then Shall Ye Shout" (before 1886):

It seems an easy thing
Mayhap one day to sing;
Yet the next day
We cannot sing or say.

Keep silence with good heart,
While silence fits our part:
Another day
We shall both sing and say.

Keep silence, counting time
To strike in at the chime:
Prepare to sound,—
Our part is coming round.

Can we not sing or say?
In silence let us pray,
And meditate
Our love-song while we wait.

[140–41]

Another poem of religious content, that elicits praise from fully a fifth of the critics of the period, is "Up-hill" (1858), a dialogue between a climbing traveler and one who is already at the place of destination:

> Does the road wind up-hill all the way?
>   Yes, to the very end.
> Will the day's journey take the whole long day?
>   From morn to night, my friend.
>
> [339]

According to the poet and critic Arthur Symons, writing in the July 1887 *London Quarterly Review,* a conservative review of contemporary belles lettres, politics, and science, Rossetti's sincere piety is nowhere better reflected than in this very verse from "Up-hill," where, as in most of her spiritual poems, she expresses "the same certainty and the same thought of relief" that she will be with God after death.[6]

Symons goes on to say that Rossetti's expressions of piety contain the intensity, devoutness, and sometimes liturgical quality of many spiritual poems of the ages; yet unlike them, her poems are never didactic, never seek to instruct. She does not preach; she "prays." Her poetry is "charged with personal emotion, a cry of the heart, and ecstasy of the soul's grief or joy." It is as if we are eavesdropping on a "dialogue of the soul with God."[7] Such awe-ful emotion he finds on ready display in "Despised and Rejected" (1864):

> 'Friend, My Feet Bleed,
> Open thy door to Me and comfort Me.'
> 'I will not open, trouble me no more.
> Go on the way footsore,
> I will not rise and open unto thee.'
> 'Then is it nothing to thee? Open, see
> Who stands to plead with thee.
> Open, lest I should pass thee by, and thou
> One day entreat my Face
> And howl for grace,
> And I be deaf as thou art now.
> Open to Me.'
>
> [241]

And the same ecstasy of a triumphant faith, Symons states, is evident in "Advent" (1858), in which, after many dark nights of

anxious waiting and watching, the vigils are over; the Bridegroom
is coming at last:

> Weeping we hold Him fast to-night;
>   We will not let Him go
> Till daybreak smite our wearied sight
>   And summer smite the snow:
> Then figs shall bud, and dove with dove
>   Shall coo the livelong day;
> Then He shall say, 'Arise, My love,
>   My fair one, come away.'

[203]

An anonymous critic for the *Saturday Review* of January 1895, a
journal of politics, literature, science, and art, concurs with Symons, but cites other examples of the poet's work to make the
point: "In [Rossetti's love and religious] poems, which are perhaps
the finest part of her work in verse, it is with a mainly tragic
ecstasy that she sends up her soul to God, out of the depths."[8]

It is a love of Christ in particular that informs Rossetti's best
poems, according to Lily Watson, a literary critic for the weekly
Sunday At Home, miscellany of an evangelistic enterprise. Witness
"A Song for the Least of All Saints" (before 1893):

> Love is the key of life and death,
>   Of hidden heavenly mystery;
> Of all Christ is, of all He saith,
>   Love is the key.
>   . . . .
> Ah, Lord, I have such feeble faith,
>   Such feeble hope to comfort me:
> But love it is, is strong as death,
>   And I love Thee.

[179]

"Christians of all shades of faith will find here something that they
can appropriate as the utterance of their own heart," Watson assures readers of the May 5, 1894, issue.[9]

Some critics focus on the mysticism—the belief that direct
knowledge of God, spiritual truth, or ultimate reality can be at-
tained through subjective experience—in Rossetti's devotional
poems. As Rossetti's mystical gifts are explained by an anonymous
reviewer for the *Saturday Review* of February 1896, the poet, having
given her heart, her genius, and her life to God, "is rewarded by

becoming a power to reveal in her verse to the weary generations of mankind the mysteries of that inmost shrine of the Christian religion where God is seen as Love and Love as God."[10]

For A. Smellie, whose works of criticism appear frequently in the *Wesleyan Methodist Magazine* devoted to matters of sectarian concern, what sets Rossetti apart from other mystics is her melancholy, for what has been revealed to her is that human lives are beset by many dangers of their own making. This message and mood, he informs readers of issue number 118 of 1896, is clearly illustrated in the poem "Who Shall Deliver Me?" (1864):

> God harden me against myself,
> This coward with pathetic voice
> Who craves for ease, and rest, and joys:
>
> Myself, arch-traitor to myself;
> My hollowest friend, my deadliest foe,
> My clog whatever road I go.
>
> Yet One there is can curb myself,
> Can roll the strangling load from me,
> Break off the yoke and set me free.
>
> [238]

But, says Smellie, "those who know the abysses know the sunlight on the mountain peaks as well," and so Rossetti sings an impassioned hymn of thanks "to Christ for His Redemption of our danger-haunted and paralyzed life."[11]

Lionel Johnson, a frequent reviewer for the *Academy*, does not call Rossetti a mystic, but his search for a way to express the "unique interest" of Rossetti's religious poems leads him to the vocabulary of mysticism. These poems he relates in the July 25, 1896 issue, "bring together all the elements of art's excellence and of a Christian faith. . . . Their unique interest is a tenderness in them, a tremulous and wistful beauty of adoration. . . . This is more than imagination, it is nothing less than vision."[12]

It is not only Rossetti's devotional poems that critics find notable for their religious ardor but a number of "general" poems as well. Often cited in this category is "The Convent Threshold" (1858). Part 1 of this dramatic monologue develops the theme of guilt and repentance; the second sets forth two dream visions that develop the theme symbolically; and the third ends in a renunciation of the speaker's earthly love and the hope that she will meet him again in heaven:

> You sinned with me a pleasant sin;
> Repent with me, for I repent.
>
> . . . .
> I tell you what I dreamed last night.
> It was not dark, it was not light,
> Cold dews had drenched my plenteous hair
> Through clay; you came to seek me there,
>
> . . . .
> To you; I answered half asleep:
> 'My pillow is damp, my sheets are red,
> There's a leaden tester to my bed:
> Find you a warmer playfellow,
> A warmer pillow for your head. . . .'

[341–42]

The speaker hopes that by giving up her earthly love, she will be rewarded after death. In heaven, "we shall meet as once we met / And love with the old familiar love."

For those reviewing "The Convent Threshold" in the secular and Protestant presses, this "passion remembered and repressed"—as an anonymous critic in the *Saturday Review* of January 1895, characterized the motif of such works—has given rise to Rossetti's best poems.[13] Another anonymous critic, for the ecumenical publication the *Ecclesiastic and Theologian* in October 1862, affirms that the poem "indicates the possession of great power on the part of its author."[14] Arthur Symons reserves the term "noble" for the poem, contending in the *London Quarterly Review*, that "the religious fervour, the personal emotion—all her noblest gifts and qualities, with her noblest possibilities of style and versification—meet here as one."[15]

Alice Meynell, poet and literary critic, goes a step further. She writes in the February 1895, *New Review*, a magazine of literature, science, politics, and art, that the sentiment expressed in "The Convent Threshold" is so moving, the feeling it conveys so urgent, that these verses prove Rossetti to be an artist. The poem, Meynell notes, is "a song of penitence for love that yet praises love more fervently than would a chorus hymeneal":[16]

> To-day, while it is called to-day,
> Kneel, wrestle, knock, do violence, pray.
>
> . . . .
> I turn from you my cheeks and eyes,
> My hair which you shall see no more—

Alas for joy that went before,

. . . .

My words were slow; my tears were few;
But through the dark my silence spoke. . . .

[341]

The *Catholic World*'s anonymous critic of October 1876, offers
a caveat: The fact that the speaker finds it painful to renounce this
"pleasant sin" makes the poet's religious ardor suspect. Unlike the
devotional poems that are committed to the love of God alone, this
poem expresses regret for the loss of wordly pleasures. True, the
critic says, the "poem contains a strong contrast—and yet how
weak a one to the truly spiritual soul!"[17]
An appreciably smaller number of critics turned their attention
to Rossetti's fantasy poems, the narrative verses evoking spirit
worlds. One such poem is "Goblin Market" (1850), the story of
two sisters, Laura and Lizzie, who are tempted by goblin merchants—malignant spirits—to partake of their luscious wares of
fruit. Laura succumbs to the temptation, eats, and sickens. Lizzie
refrains but, in a spirit of self-sacrifice, daringly meets the "fruit
merchant men" again to bring back a cure for her sister's condition: a second taste of the evil fruit. Laura tastes again, finds it like
"wormwood," and is restored to health. And, indeed, according to
Mackenzie Bell's reckoning in *Christina Rossetti: A Biographical
and Critical Study* (1898), " 'The Goblin Market' remains . . . the
most genuinely popular of all Christina Rossetti's writings."[18]
Popular, yes, but where the critics are concerned, the response is
mixed. Rossetti's fusing of the real and the unreal, and the imagery
and rhythms employed for this task, has created a new world that
critics in the liberal secular and religious press delight in, if not
fully understand. Among those writing for the conservative presses, secular and religious, however, there appears a disposition to
dismiss such novel worlds out of hand; any attempt at creating
them is doomed to fail.
Among the nay-sayers is an anonymous critic for the October
1893 issue of the conservative *Edinburgh Review,* a monthly offering fiction, travel, history, poetry, biography, and current affairs.
According to this reviewer, the poem has an "element of the
grotesque and disproportionate in it," that makes the two girls
"like the figures in Dante Rossetti's pictures, inhuman and unreal."[19]

The anonymous critic, for the October 1862 *Ecclesiastic and Theologian* finds fault with the poem's "careless" construction.[20] And F. A. Rudd, a leading critic for the *Catholic World*, calls it the worst poem of the volume *Goblin Market and Other Poems* (1862). His judgment in the March 1867, issue is harsh:

> For imagination, she offers fantasy; for sentiment, sentimentality; for aspiration, ambition; for originality and thought, little or nothing; for melody, fantastic jangling of words; and these with all tenderness for the ill-starred intensity of purpose that could fetch them so far, are no more poetry than the industrious Colonists' shiploads of mica were gold."[21]

Among the yea-sayers—about three-quarters of the critics who reviewed "Goblin Market"—R. R. Bowker's assessment is typical. Despite its "weird Mysticism," the founder of the general interest *Harper's New Monthly Magazine* writes in its issue of May 1888, "Goblin Market is also a poem of "singular sweetness."[22] Symons adds in his *London Quarterly Review* piece that the witchcraft is so "subtle" that Rossetti seems to bewitch both herself and us without intending to do either. Her merging of the matter-of-fact with the fantastic and bewildering, he states, produces the effect of the supernatural, and we are made to believe everything. It is "as fresh and as strange as the dreams of childhood."[23]

The critic James B. Kenyon, writing in the *Methodist Review* of theology and religion in September 1896, views the poem as a "bizarre fantasy wrought out with the utmost adroitness."[24] Christabel Coleridge, a critic with family ties to Samuel Taylor Coleridge, writes in the *Monthly Packet* for March 1895, a general interest magazine, that the poem is "as unaccountable and absolute a vision as 'Kubla Khan' itself." She believes that there is no use in trying to make out the exact meaning of every detail; some are as inconsequential as those in a "real legend or tradition."[25]

The critic Mrs. Charles Eliot Norton, writing in the September 1863, issue of *Macmillan's Magazine* of literature, history, travel, politics, and manners—one of the first periodicals to accept from their contributors only signed articles—considers that the poem "vies with Coleridge's 'Ancient Mariner' in its degree for the vivid and wonderful power by which things unreal and mystic are made to blend and link themselves with the every day images and events of common life."[26]

Edmund Gosse, a prominent critic who collaborated on the *Illustrated Record of English Literature* (1903–4), also took up his pen in praise of "Goblin Market." In the *Century Magazine* for June 1893, a popular illustrated journal of literature, biography, science, and art, he compares "its witty and fantastic conception . . . embroidered with fancies, descriptions, peals of laughing music" to a "queer Japanese figure . . . clothed with brocade, making the entire effect beautiful and harmonious without having ceased to be grotesque."[27]

"The Prince's Progress" (1861–65), another long narrative poem, reviewed by half of Rossetti's nineteenth-century critics, tells of yet another corner of the fairy world. The poem relates the tale of a handsome, indolent youth, who sets out tardily on a voyage to see his beloved and loiters in evil company by the way. He is lured by casual loves and monetary concerns, and, upon finally reaching his long-patient betrothed, finds her dead. "There is an elusiveness about its magic," Symons notes, "making familiar things look strange, and weaving and unweaving its spells beneath our eyes."[28] He calls attention to the magical glitter of the milk-maid's eyes as she casts her spell over the errant Prince:

> Was it milk now, or was it cream?
> Was she a maid, or an evil dream?
> Her eyes began to glitter and gleam;
>   He would have gone, but he stayed instead;
> Green they gleamed as he looked in them:
>   'Give me my fee,' she said.—
>
> [27]

Although most critics prefer "Goblin Market" to "The Prince's Progress," Alice Law stands with the minority. Her evaluation, published in April 1895, in the *Westminster Review*— an "organ of the free-thinkers" founded by John Stuart Mill—is that "Miss Rossetti's subtle and mysterious art finds its most perfect expression in 'The Prince's Progress'" because of its "atmosphere of old-world charm and mysticism."[29]

Another type of Rossetti work infused with supernaturalism, the ghost poems, interests far fewer critics and inspires less passionate opinion. The tone of these poems is melancholy, the scene sepulchral. In "The Hour and the Ghost" (1856), the ghost of a dead lover returns, on the day of her wedding with someone else, to the lady who has jilted him, in the hope of taking her to his

home beyond the grave. The woman pleads with her new bridegroom to hold her fast:

> *Bride*
> Hold me one moment longer!
> He taunts me with the past,
> His clutch is waxing stronger;
> Hold me fast, hold me fast.
> He draws me from thy heart,
> And I cannot withhold:
> He bids my spirit depart
> With him into the cold:—
> Oh bitter vows of old!

Despite her terrified cries, the ghost takes his revenge:

> *Ghost*
> O fair frail sin,
> O poor harvest gathered in!
> Thou shalt visit him again
> To watch his heart grow cold:
> To know the gnawing pain
> I knew of old;
> To see one much more fair
> Fill up the vacant chair,
> Fill his heart, his children bear;
> While thou and I together,
> In the outcast weather,
> Toss and howl and spin.

[326–27]

Symons, for example, calls these "strange little poems, with
their sombre and fantastic colouring—the picturesque outcome of
deep and curious ponderings on things unseen."[30] The anonymous
Catholic World (1876) critic, for his part, is content to register
good-humored dismay at the ill-mannered ghost Rossetti has
drawn: "We should imagine that the ghost would have grown
wiser, if not more charitable, by his visit to the other world, and
would show himself quite willing to throw at least the ghost of a
slipper after the happy pair."[31]

In "The Poor Ghost" (1863), a dead lover returns to her earthly
fiancé with the intention of taking him with her beyond the grave.
But he tells her that her death has ended their relationship and begs
her to go back without him:

'Indeed I loved you, my chosen friend,
I loved you for life, but life has an end;
Through sickness I was ready to tend:
But death mars all, which we cannot mend.

'Indeed I loved you; I love you yet,
If you will stay where your bed is set,
Where I have planted a violet,
Which the wind waves, which the dew makes wet.'

'Life is gone, then love too is gone,
It was a reed that I leant upon:
Never doubt I will leave you alone
And not wake you rattling bone with bone.

'I go home alone to my bed
Dug deep at the foot and deep at the head,
Roofed in with a load of lead,
Warm enough for the forgotten dead.'

[360]

The poet's ghosts, Symons says, are not brought back by
seances; they are serious dead men and women who come back
again in the spirit. He finds that Rossetti "cares intimately" about
knowing and seeing what is going on in the minds of the de-
parted.[32]

An anonymous critic for the *Saturday Review* of January 1895,
who looked back on the Rossetti poems in the year following the
poet's death, concluded that she could write not only verses "of
vivid sincerity, of downright passion, of religious conviction, but
also of fantastic subtlety, of airy grace, of remote and curious
charm."[33] Witness "a child's quaint familiarity with the impossible" in "Goblin Market," and "the child's terror and attraction"
in her ghost poems in which dead people try vainly and desperately
to resume their earthly existence.

Almost all of the critics who address Rossetti's work in this
period concern themselves with the themes of her poems. They
discern these to be love—romantic and spiritual—death, and love
intertwined with death, noting the various treatments these themes
receive. Yet rarely do Rossetti's verses sing of happy love. When
they do, they are received by critics as a welcome relief from the
melancholy strain that prevails in most of her poetry. Bell, for
example, finds "Maiden-Song" (1873) "exquisite love poetry . . .
full of joy and unshadowed by grief—so full of joy, indeed that for

this reason alone, it stands out pre-eminently among its author's best work."[34] Margaret, the heroine,

> Sang a golden-bearded King
>   Straightway to her feet,
> Sang him silent where he knelt
>   In eager anguish sweet,
> But when the clear voice died away,
>   When longest echoes died,
> He stood up like a royal man
>   And claimed her for his bride.
> So three maids were wooed and won
>   In a brief May-tide,
> Long ago and long ago.
>
> [41]

Harry Baxton Foreman, witnessing a similar joy, sees it cloaked in a becoming reticence. He writes in the August 1869, issue of *Tinsley's Magazine,* a mixture of literary and antiquarian matters and fanciful prose and verse, that the lines of the love lyric "A Birthday" (1857) are suffused with the "healthy happiness and the ringing melody of a joyful heart . . . the very essence of maiden delicacy."

> The birthday of my life
> Is come, my love is come to me.
>
> [335]

To the poet's credit, says Foreman, the happiness does not break forth in an "unmeasured and uncomely burst . . . of excessive openness of expression," that is "distasteful to readers of average delicacy." He considers Rossetti's "reticence in songs of the affections . . . a gift of great price."[35]

In the same poem, a reviewer for the February 1895 *National Review,* a journal of politics, arts, and science, detects not modesty but its opposite. Arthur Christopher Benson, novelist and student of literature, notes that "very occasionally [Rossetti] allowed herself, in the early days, to speak of love with the generous abandon of an ardent spirit."[36]

Critics note another variation on the theme of love in the sonnet "A Triad" (1856), a contrasting of three women. The first, like a honey-sweetened bee, drones rich and fat on love; the second, a "sluggish wife," smooth and soft as a "tinted hyacinth," grows "gross in soulless love"; the third, a virgin, "blue with famine after love," finally dies for the lack of it:

> Three sang of love together: one with lips
> 　　Crimson with cheeks and bosom in a glow,
> Flushed to the yellow hair and finger-tips;
> 　　And one there sang who soft and smooth as snow
> 　　Bloomed like a tinted hyacinth at a show;
> And one was blue with famine after love,
> 　　Who like a harpstring snapped rang harsh and low
> The burden of what those were singing of.
>
> 　　　　　　　　　　　　　　　　　[329]

Gosse's *Century Magazine* review calls "A Triad" a marvelous objective sonnet because here Rossetti's "touch is most firm and picturesque, her intelligence most weighty, and her style most completely characteristic."[37]

Rossetti's theme of love interwoven with death evokes still other responses from critics. For Benson, such poems are marked by a brooding quality: "As a rule her thoughts of love are clouded by some dark sense of loss, of having missed the satisfaction that the hungering soul might claim."[38] He cites as an example "When I am Dead, My Dearest" (1848):

> When I am dead, my dearest,
> 　　Sing so sad songs for me;
> Plant thou no roses at my head,
> 　　Nor shady cypress trees:
> Be the green grass above me
> 　　With showers and dewdrops wet:
> And if thou wilt, remember,
> 　　And if thou wilt, forget.
>
> I shall not see the shadows.
> 　　I shall not feel the rain;
> I shall not hear the nightingale
> 　　Sing on as if in pain:
> And dreaming through the twilight
> 　　That doth not rise nor set,
> Haply I may remember,
> 　　And haply may forget.
>
> 　　　　　　　　　　　　　　　[290–91]

Symons believes that the peculiar charm of these poems in which love and death are intertwined is their lyrical quality and their "thoughtfulness that broods as well as sees, and has, like shadowed water, its mysterious depths"—both evident in "An End" (1849):

> Love, strong as Death, is dead.
> Come, let us make his bed
> Among the dying flowers:
> A green turf at his head;
> And a stone at his feet,
> Where we may sit
> In the quiet evening hours.
>
> [292]

Symons, on his part, suggests what has led Rossetti to write such works as these:

> The thought of death has a constant fascination for Rossetti, almost such a fascination as it had for Leopardi or Baudelaire; only it is not the fascination of attraction, as with the one, or of the repulsion, as with the other; but of *interest,* sad but unquiet interest: interest in what the dead are doing underground, in their memories—if memory they have—of the world they have left; a singular, whimsical *sympathy* with the poor dead.[39]

As a telling example of this he offers "After Death" (1849):

> The curtains were half drawn, the floor was swept
>   And strewn with rushes, rosemary and may
>   Lay thick upon the bed on which I lay,
> Where through the lattice ivy-shadows crept.
> He leaned above me, thinking that I slept
>   And could not hear him; but I heard him say,
>   'Poor child, poor child': and as he turned away
> Came a deep silence, and I knew he wept.
> He did not touch the shroud, or raise the fold
>   That hid my face, or take my hand in his,
>   Or ruffle the smooth pillows for my head:
>   He did not love me living; but once dead
>   He pitied me; and very sweet it is
> To know he still is warm though I am cold.
>
> [292–93]

In poems that contemplate death itself, critics perceive a different mood at work. Alice Law states that in "Dream Land" (1849), Rossetti joyfully anticipated the thought of death and dwelt upon it as the prospect of eternal, soothing peace. "Death had no terrors

for her; it was to her but as cool, refreshing sleep." She envies the
dead "because they are estranged from all material things":[40]

> Where sunless rivers weep
> Their waves into the deep,
> She sleeps a charmed sleep:
>   Awake her not
>
> . . . .
>
> Rest, rest, a perfect rest
> Shed over brow and breast;
> Her face is toward the west,
>   The purple land.
>
> . . . .
>
> Rest, rest, for evermore
> Upon a mossy shore;
> Rest, rest at the heart's core
>   Till time shall cease:
> Sleep that no pain shall wake;
> Night that no morn shall break,
> Till joy shall overtake
>   Her perfect peace.
>
> [292]

Almost a third of the critics are concerned with placing Rossetti's verses in a poetic tradition. They note the resemblance of her
sonnets to those poets of her own era and of past ages. An anonymous reviewer for the September 1881, *Athenaeum*, a journal of
literature, science, and the arts, states, for example, that in the
Monna Innominata sonnets (before 1882) Rossetti has been able
"to import into the regular form more of the Shakespearean
sweetness than can perhaps be found in any other poet, not even
excepting Hartley Coleridge [son of Samuel Taylor Coleridge]."[41]

An anonymous critic for the November 5, 1887, *Literary World*,
a review of the arts, compares Rossetti's poetry to Dante
Alighieri's and Petrarch's and notes that "through the whole, there
breathes the purest and most unselfish devotion." The critic adds
that "even Mrs. Browning's sonnets, disguised as translations from
the Portuguese, are less beautiful in form, less self-forgetful in
spirit than these."[42] He particularly commends Sonnet 12 of the
Monna Innominata series, which has interested perhaps a third of
Rossetti's critics. Here a young woman assures her beloved of an
affection so strong that, should he find someone to take her place,
she would not begrudge him this happiness:

If there be any one who can take my place
  And make you happy whom I grieve to grieve,
  Think not that I can grudge it, but believe
I do commend you to that nobler grace,
That readier wit than mine, that sweeter face;
  Yea, since your riches make me rich, conceive
  I too am crowned, while bridal crowns I weave,
And thread the bridal dance with jocund pace
For if I did not love you, it might be
  That I should grudge you some one dear delight;
    But since the heart is yours that was mine own
Your pleasure is my pleasure, right my right,
Your honourable freedom makes me free,
  And you companioned I am not alone.

[63]

T. Hall Caine, in the August 1881, issue of the *Academy,* concurs: "Tenderness more true, and resignation more beautiful, . . . do not find utterances in English poetry"[43] more selfless than in Sonnet 12.

Benson notes that Rossetti's poetry contains "the balanced simplicity" without the "elaborate conceit" of George Herbert, the seventeenth-century religious poet, and has none of the "desperate euphemism"—the elegant artificiality of language—of Richard Crashaw or the "pathetic refinement" of Henry Vaughan, both contemporaries of Herbert. Her puritan outlook, Benson claims, "even surpasses that of Charles Wesley—one of the great hymn-makers of the eighteenth century—and her divine ardor that of Cardinal John Henry Newman."[44]

An unnamed critic for the *Saturday Review's* February 1896, issue informs reader that "compared with her, John Keble [another religious poet and essayist, and coinitiator, with Newman, of the Oxford Movement] is simply a careful, laborious and commendable hymn-maker with some feeling for nature, but very little insight into the human heart." Furthermore, had George Herbert been a modern, he would be "fairly measured with her"; and at his "rare best [Henry] Vaughan most nearly matches her highest. But the intensity of her religious emotion belongs to herself alone."[45]

Gosse is of a similar mind: "As a religious poet of our time she has no rival but Cardinal Newman, and it could only be schismatic prejudice or absence of critical faculty which would deny her a place, as a poet, higher than that of our exquisite master of prose."[46]

Chambers, writing in a later issue of the *Academy*, sees an affinity between Rossetti and the Dante of *The Divine Comedy*, "whether she elects the traditional inheritance of religious poet, the well-worn store of scriptural metaphor, rich with its association, or whether she goes further afield to seek a spiritual suggestion in the harvest of her own eye."[47]

The mood of Rossetti's religious poems, Symons says, reminds him of the work of Donne and Herbert: Like them, Rossetti "will find place for some quaint conceit," even in poems that reflect a deep mood, "startling us perhaps by its profound and unthought-of naturalness,"[48] such as in the poem "Advent" (1858):

> This Advent moon shines cold and clear,
>   These Advent nights are long;
> Our lamps have burned year after year
>   And still their flame is strong.
> 'Watchman, what of the night?' we cry,
>   Heart-sick with hope deferred;
> 'No speaking signs are in the sky,'
>   Is still the watchman's world.
>
>   . . . .
> We weep because the night is long,
>   We laugh for day shall rise,
> We sing a slow contented song
>   And knock at Paradise.
> Weeping we hold Him fast Who wept
>   for us, we hold Him fast;
> And will not let Him go except
>   He bless us first or last.
>
> [202]

Bayard Taylor, author of *Critical Essays and Literary Notes* (1880), considers Rossetti to lack the "brilliancy of rhetoric, rhythmical movement and . . . intensity and vividness of apprehension" of Jean Ingelow; yet "she is simpler, more natural and unstudied, more . . . direct in her appeals to sentiment and feeling, and more purely devotional in her nature"—hence her wide popularity. He recognizes, however, that "the reader will set this or that higher, according to the taste which is born of his spiritual temperament.[49]

A few critics detect a Romantic influence in Rossetti's poems. Symons, for example, notes a similarity between "The Prince's Progress" and the Romantic ballads of William Morris, the nineteenth-century designer and craftsman. And more:

The narrative is in the pure romantic spirit. . . . One episode—that of the old man in the cavern among the furnaces, brewing the Elixir of Life which is to snatch him from death's door, and dying, with one foot already on the threshold of immortality—is like a picture of Goya or Callot.[50]

Alice Law remarks of the same poem: "We seem to breathe the very atmosphere of old-world charm and mysticism," which she sees as a mark of the Pre-Raphaelites. "The stanzas, as it were, exhale that almost indescribable aesthetic aroma of mingled flowers and herbs—rosemarry, thyme, rue, and languorous lilies":

> Till all sweet gums and juices flow,
> Till the blossom of blossoms blow,
> The long hours go and come and go;
>   The bride she sleepeth, waketh, sleepeth,
> Waiting for one whose coming is slow:—
>   Hark! the bride weepeth.

[26]

Rossetti's description of the dead bride, Law says, gives one the impression of tasting and smelling the heavy embalming odors in the oppressive atmosphere of the royal chamber of death:

> What is this that comes through the door,
> The face covered, the feet before?
>   This that coming takes his breath;
> This Bride not seen, to be seen no more
>   Save of Bridegroom Death?

[34]

These verses, Law continues, have "the deep medieval colouring, and quaint bejewelled setting of an old thirteenth- or fourteenth-century manuscript," as is also seen "in the works of her brother and the other Pre-Raphaelites."[51]

For *National Review* critic Benson, it is "A Birthday" (1857) that most vividly reflects "the pictorial splendours of the Pre-Raphaelite school":[52]

> My heart is like a singing bird
>   Whose nest is in a watered shoot:
> My heart is like an apple-tree
>   Whose boughs are bent with thickset fruit;
> My heart is like a rainbow shell

That paddles in a halcyon sea;
My heart is gladder than all these
Because my love is come to me.

[335]

Richard Le Gallienne, a noted critic and man of letters, writing in the *Academy* for February 7, 1891, also sees Pre-Raphaelite tendencies in "A Birthday." He discerns in the poem the same strain of mystic materialism that runs through the verses of Rossetti's brother Dante Gabriel—the same "decorative quality, as of sumptuous needle-work designs in rich cloth, which is like a painter's poetry in its rich material symbolism." He says that the poem, "like the Song of Solomon," throbs with life and heartfelt happiness:[53]

Raise me a dais of silk and down;
    Hang it with vair and purple dyes;
Carve it in doves and pomegranates,
    And peacocks with a hundred eyes;
Work it in gold and silver grapes,
    In leaves and silver fleurs-de-lys;
Because the birthday of my life
Is come, my love is come to me.

[335]

Rossetti's affinity with the artistic creations of her brother is also noted by Law in discussing "Goblin Market." She states that the vividness of the goblin fruits compares with "that pure, warm ecstasy of early Italian colouring which Rossetti's brush has immortalized for us":[54]

'Look at our apples
Russet and dun,
Bob at our cherries,
Bite at our peaches,
Citrons and dates,
Grapes for the asking,
Pears red with basking
Out in the sun,
Plums on their twigs;
Pluck them and suck them,—
Pomegranates, figs.'

[6]

Pre-Raphaelite tendencies in Rossetti's ghost poems, too, are commented upon by several critics. For instance, the October 1876, *Catholic World's* anonymous reviewer calls Rossetti the literary "Queen of the Preraphaelite school" in England. The Pre-Raphaelites, this reviewer notes, "positively revel in gloom," and their favorite companions "are wan ghosts." "A favorite trick of a Preraphaelite ghost is to stalk into his old haunts, only to discover that after all people live in much in the same style as when he was in the flesh,"[55] and points out that Rossetti's ghosts take us on several such visits. One illustration is provided in "The Ghost's Petition" (1864):

> There came a footstep climbing the stair:
>   Some one standing out on the landing
> Shook the door like a puff of air—
>
> Shook the door and in he passed.
>   Did he enter? In the room centre
> Stood her husband: the door shut fast.

> [364]

With one rather long sweep of a pen, Harry Baxton Foreman firmly identifies Christina Rossetti with the Pre-Raphaelites and compares her voice with that of Elizabeth Barrett Browning. Both remarks, made in a general discussion of the character of male and female literary artists, are included in an article on the Rossetti's prepared for *Tinsley's Magazine*.

> Logical reasons could be adduced, no doubt, why it is not only improbable, but impossible, that women should obtain supremacy, for instance, in epic poetry, in the drama, in sculpture, in musical composition; and this, perhaps, on the ground that women's minds are so differently fashioned from men's, that they could not possibly be brought to the severe task in analysis and synthesis, and the protracted stress and strain, which extended works in these *genre* demand . . . doubtless it is logic; but fortunately logic is not everything.[56]

And further:

> Although [Rossetti] has not produced any one work of great dimensions, or even of great scope in small dimensions, her two little volumes yet constitute not only a very choice aggregation or real poetry, but also a significant fact in the history of female literature. Miss Rossetti shows before all things that a woman of esthetic genius is

not necessarily a wayward *fabricante* of whatever matter comes into her head for artistic manipulation, but that a woman may be trained to a special manner of workmanship, and made amenable to the influences of a movement just as unmistakably as a man may.[57]

Later in the article, in comparing Rossetti with another Victorian poet, Elizabeth Barrett Browning, Forman argues that although the popular author of "Sonnets from the Portuguese" has a larger caliber of mind, superior powers of expression, and greater ability than Rossetti has,

[Mrs. Browning] has not shown, with all her impassioned bursts and sweet outpourings, which attain perfection by force of passion or sweetness, the *sense* that poetic manipulation is a requisite of art; and Miss Christina Rossetti, without this sweeping force of passion, with a more limited range of emotional manifestation, and with a far narrower area of subject, has unquestionably shown this sense. Therefore to her be all honour for being the first to show what, in this behalf, may be achieved by an apt and fitting education.[58]

Foreman seems to be saying that women can do things as well as men can, but it would disturb a lot of people if they did. Having taken exception to an oral remark of Mrs. Browning's about the encumbrance of Victorian female fashions—"This vile woman's way of trailing garments shall not trip me up."—he considers her "impassioned bursts" to be "pardonable" though "ungratifying." By her utterance she "disarranges the stately folds of a woman's rainment more than we would choose to have them disarranged." How different from Christina Rossetti, who, with her "purified essence of purity," would never make such an unladylike statement.[59]

Rossetti's nature poems are compared with those of nature poets of past eras, and the critics of this period are almost unanimous in assessing hers to be as poetic and musical as those of the most famous lyricists of literary history. Alice Law compares these nature poems to those of the great Caroline lyricist Robert Herrick—"We seem to hear the inner voice of Nature, as of man, uttered through the imperishable medium of a highly finished and delicate art"—and their melodious notes to those of a bird, in their richness and in their spontaneity "pure and clear as the freshly bubbling waters of a spring."[60] Law believes that "Spring" (1859) is similar to many of Herrick's poems that emphasize the vanity of all earthly things:

There is no time like Spring that passes by,
Now newly born, and now
Hastening to die.

[346]

Christabel Coleridge points out that in Rossetti's nature poems there is intense delight in beauty and, every now and then, a hint of that "love of small quaint things which is so characteristic a note of the greatest of her poems." She sees a similarity between Rossetti's work and that of her own kin, Samuel Taylor Coleridge, because Rossetti loved "all things both great and small,"[61] as is amply demonstrated in the verses from *Sing-Song* (1872), a book for children:

A motherless soft lambkin
    Alone upon a hill;
No mother's fleece to shelter him
    And wrap him from the cold:—
I'll run to him and comfort him,
    I'll fetch him, that I will;
I'll care for him and feed him
    Until he's strong and bold.

[433]

Mackenzie Bell compares the verses in *Sing-Song* with the best of Robert Louis Stevenson's *Garden of Verses*. Rossetti's are "as realistic in the higher sense as the best poems" in Stevenson's volume, all "while full of a dramatic imagination that lifts them to a higher level of insight and aspiration than is reached even by that delightful writer."[62] He states, however, that lines like the following might well be beyond a child's comprehension:

Hope is like a harebell trembling from its birth,
Love is like a rose the joy of all the earth;
Faith is like a lily lifted high and white,
Love is like a lovely rose the world's delight;
Harebells and sweet lilies show a thornless growth,
But the rose with all its thorns excels them both.

[428]

Symons praises these little nursery rhymes in *Sing-Song* for their musical quality, their freshness, glowing brightness, thoughtfulness, and spontaneity. Such poetry, he says, "evades analysis; we could as easily dissect a butterfly's wing. It is simply a child's

mood, a child's fancies and ideas set to song." The serious-
ness of the mood in some of them is "like the voice of a wise elder
who is still a child at heart, and among children." Symons also
notes "a careful absence of emphasis, a subdued colour and
calculated vagueness" that give a particular tone to Rossetti's
songs—"ethereal and quintessential," as perfect as those lyrics of
Shelley, "whom she resembles also in her free but flawless treatment of rhythm":[63]

> Who has seen the wind?
>   Neither I nor you:
> But when the leaves hang trembling
>   The wind is passing thro'.
>
> Who has seen the wind?
>   Neither you nor I:
> But when the trees bow down their heads
>   The wind is passing by.
>
>   [438]

And again here:

> When a mounting skylark sings
>   In the sunlit summer morn,
> I know that heaven is up on high,
>   And on earth are fields of corn.
>
> But when a nightingale sings
>   In the moonlit summer even,
> I know not if earth is merely earth,
>   Only that heaven is heaven.
>
>   [438]

William Michael Rossetti notes in his "Memoir" to the *Poetical
Works of Christina Rossetti* (1903) that "up to the time of her death
little was publicly known about her, as she had led an extremely
quiet and even secluded life." Still, some 40 percent of those who
review his sister's work reflect upon the relation of Rossetti's passionate poetry to events in her life. Lacking biographical data in
the years before 1898, when Mackenzie Bell's *Christina Rossetti: A
Biographical and Critical Study* appeared, they could only surmise
that she wrote from personal experience.

Even after Bell's revelations, elicited from William Michael, that
Christina had refused to marry the two men who courted her—
James Collinson, the Pre-Raphaelite painter, because he had con-

Head of Christina Rossetti. From the pencil drawing by Dante Gabriel Rossetti, 1848.

verted to Catholicism; and the scholar Charles Bagot Cayley, because she found his faith "woefully defective"[64]—they discretely refrain from asserting specifics.

Benson, for example, limns Rossetti's biography in these general terms in 1895:

> Miss Rossetti's poems are so passionately human a document as to set one tracing by a sort of inevitable instinct the secrets of a buoyant and tender soul, sharpened and refined by blow after blow of harsh discipline. The same autobiographical savour haunts all her work as haunted the later dramas of Charlotte Bronte. . . . Step by step it reveals itself, the sad and stately development of this august soul. The first tremulous outlook upon the intolerable loveliness of life, the fantastic melancholy of youth, the deep desire of love, the drawing nearer of the veiled start, disappointment, disillusionment, the overpowering rush of melancholy that had waited like a beast in ambush, for moments of lassitude and reaction. Then was the crisis: would the wounded life creep on a broken wing, or would the spiritual vitality suffice to fill the intolerable void? It did suffice: and the character that thus found repose was attested by the rational and temperate form of faith that ministered to the failing soul.[65]

He sees in the sad illusions of her sonnet "Remember" (1849) a hungering spirit, the loss of hope. It is especially in this poem, Benson says, that "the soul-history is written in plain characters":[66]

> Remember me when I am gone away,
>   Gone far away into the silent land;
>   When you can no more hold me by the hand,
> Nor I half turn to go yet turning stay.
> Remember me when no more day by day
>   You tell me of our future that you plann'd:
>   Only remember me; you understand
> It will be late to counsel then or pray.
> Yet if you should forget me for a while
>   And afterwards remember, do not grieve:
>   For if the darkness and corruption leave
>   A vestige of the thoughts that once I had,
> Better by far you should forget and smile
>   Than that you should remember and be sad.

[294]

Another reviewer in 1895 is willing to go a bit further. The heroine of "The Prince's Progress"—she who died of a broken heart because her indolent fiancé took so long in coming to claim her—is Rossetti herself. Alice Law, like Benson, then offers a general spiritual biography of the poet—and provides, along the way, a woman's-eye-view of Victorian womanhood:

> We hear the song of her overflowing heart, longing to spend and to be spent for love. There is nothing modern about the singing, unless it be its hopelessness, throughout that of the old-world heroine—pensive, clinging, passive.

Law theorizes that here, as in the poem "Twice" (1864), Rossetti "found consolation for the unsatisfied yearnings of the heart in devout prostration of spirit, and the uplifting of the soul to God."[67] Symons's reading of "Twice," however, is different from Law's. He sees not prostration but passion; Rossetti is giving expression "to the suppressed bitterness of a disappointed heart, anguish of unuttered passion reaching to a point of ascetic abnegation, a devout frenzy of patience, which is the springing of the bitter seed of hope dead in a fiery martyrdom":[68]

> You took my heart in your hand
> With a friendly smile,
> With a critical eye you scanned,
> Then set it down,
> And said: It is still unripe,
> Better wait awhile;
> Wait while the skylarks pipe,
> Till the corn grows brown.
>
> As you set it down it broke—
> Broke, but I did not wince;
> I smiled at the speech you spoke,
> At your judgment that I heard:
> But I have not often smiled
> Since then, nor questioned since,
> Nor cared for corn-flowers wild,
> Nor sung with the singing bird.

[366]

William Michael Rossetti's 1896 publication of *New Poems*, which contained those of Christina's verses that for unknown reasons she had declined to publish in her lifetime or had withdrawn from future editions of her works, stimulated additional criticism in a biographical vein. For example, an anonymous reviewer for

the October 1896, London *Quarterly Review* claims that the
verses illuminated the momentous events in the poet's life. The
Italian poems of *Il Rosseggiar del Oriente* (1862–76) especially
reveal "the inmost thought of a pure, impassioned heart, willing
. . . to renounce every hope of earthly happiness," but unwilling to
give up hope that she and her lover will be reunited in the Paradise
of God. "Feeling half-guilty of intrusion into holy secrets and yet
welcoming the disclosure," this anonymous critic notes that Rossetti's Italian verses have no touch of bitterness in her renunciation: "The feeling that suffuses them has the deep glow of purify-
ing fire; it is something strong as death, and deathless as the
soul."[69]

An anonymous reviewer for the April 1896, issue of the *Edinburgh Review* finds "Look on This Picture and on This" (1856)—
in which a sadistic male taunts the woman he has rejected—the best
poem of the volume:[70]

> You have seen her hazel eyes, her
> warm dark skin,
> Dark hair—but oh those hazel eyes
> a devil is dancing in:—
> You, my saint, lead up to heaven,
> she lures down to sin.

But then the lover, in a tenderer mood, acknowledges that although he has found another, he still loves his deserted mistress:

> For after all I love you, loved you
> then, I love you yet:
> Listen, love, I love you: see, the
> seal of truth is set
> On my face, in tears—you cannot
> see? then feel them wet.
>
> [324–25]

W. M. Payne, writing in the April, 1896, issue of the *Dial*,
particularly likes "Introspective" (1857), another poem reflecting
intense, soul-shattering emotions. He calls it "noble" and illustra-
tive of Christina's "precocious genius":[71]

> I wish it were over the terrible pain,
> Pang after pang again and again:
> First the shattering ruining blow,

Then the probing steady and slow.
. . . .
Dumb I was when the ruin fell,
Dumb I remain and will never tell;
O my soul, I talk with thee,
But not another the sight must see.

[331]

Even before the appearance of *New Poems,* Benson had reviewed a few of the verses it contained that had appeared in early editions of the poet's works, only to be withdrawn from subsequent editions. Was it the potential for such readings of a "soul's history" that had led Christina Rossetti to suppress these works?

Benson notes of the poem "Echo" (1854) that "the veil of some pathetic possibility unfulfilled is drawn reverently aside, and the soul's history is written in plain character": "The hand that was held out in hope for the heavenly bread [was] closed upon a stone." We see that the surrender of love on earth is accepted, but the thought of what could have been is always present. The voice in "Echo" pleads:

Come back to me in dreams, that I may give
Pulse for pulse, breath for breath:
Speak low, lean low,
As long ago, my love, how long ago.

[314]

As for the ballads "Sister Maude" (circa 1860) and "Noble Sisters" (1860), Benson states, these "are but the outworks and bastions of the inner life."[72] In "Sister Maude" the speaker resents her sister's cruel meddling in her love affair and curses her for bringing shame to herself and death to her lover:

Who told my mother of my shame,
Who told my father of my dear?
Oh who but Maude, my sister Maude,
Who lurked to spy and peer.

Cold he lies, as cold as stone,
With his clotted curls about his face:
The comeliest corpse in all the world
And worthy of a queen's embrace.

[348]

But the temptation to read further biographical detail into Rossetti's works is resisted by Benson in explicit terms. He does not approve of attempts to relate or consider of any positive value the personal experiences of literary figures to their work:

> One could almost wish that Christina Rossetti were farther removed by time and space, and had passed beyond the region of letters, biographies, and personal memoirs, which before long will possibly begin "to tear her heart before the crown." Nowadays, in the excessive zest for personal information, which received such shameful incentives from Carlyle, and still more shameless encouragement from his biographers, we may thank God, like Tennyson, that there are yet poets of whom we know as little as we know of Shakespeare, about whom even the utmost diligence of researchers has disinterred but a handful of sordid and humiliating facts.[73]

Rossetti's use of *allegory,* especially as a didactic tool, interests more than half of the critics in the Victorian period. Smellie points out in the *Wesleyan Methodist,* for instance, that the poet's "constant picture of the Christian on earth is the picture of the pilgrim. His life has been quickened by Christ's great salvation. It is rendered gracious and fruitful by the love for Him which controls it."[74] For Rossetti, Smellie recognizes, it is not the perfect life. She awaits the crowning day when she will be in heaven—and as she waits she sings—as in one of her verses from *New Jerusalem and Its Citizens,* "Jerusalam Is Built of Gold" (circa 1877):

> Jerusalem, where song nor gem
>   Nor fruit nor waters cease,
> God bring us to Jerusalem,
>   God bring us home in peace;
> The strong who stand, the weak who fall,
> The first and last, the great and small,
> Home one by one, home one and all.
>
> [206]

An anonymous reviewer in the June 23, 1866, *Athenaeum* compares "The Prince's Progress" and "Goblin Market," considering each an allegorical conception of temptation. In the second, temptation is resisted by one of the sisters; in the first, temptations seduce the Prince.[75]

Some years later, in September 1881, another anonymous critic for the *Athenaeum* says that "Miss Rossetti in her strong leaning toward the allegorical view of nature and human life is a prominent figure." He calls attention to her masquelike poem, "The Months: A Pageant" (1879), which personifies January, March, July, August, October, and December as boys and February, April, May, June, September, and November as girls. This critic notes that "unlike her other allegories, however, the poem seems to inculcate no distinct moral lesson. . . . All the lesson to be drawn from it is that Nature is beautiful in her every mood and that God is good."[76]

Imagery in Rossetti's poetry concerns somewhat short of half the critics. Symons notes the concreteness of the imagery of the seasons, particularly the word-picture of springtime; one can almost smell the country air and the flowers and fruit in the verses. He observes that Rossetti never refers to mountain scenery and only rarely to the sea but delights in giving lovingly minute pictures of flowers, corn, birds, and animals,[77] as in the poem, "A Year's Windfall" (1863):

> In the wind of windy March
>   The catkins drop down,
> Curly, caterpillar-like,
>   Curious green and brown.
> With concourse of nest-building birds
>   And leaf-buds by the way,
> We begin to think of flowers
>   And life and nuts some day.
>
> [356]

Benson praises Rossetti's descriptions of the beauties of the English countryside: "The dewy English woodland, the sharp silences of winter, the gloom of low-hung clouds, and the sign of weeping rains are her backgrounds." He says that she has the power of creating "a species of aerial landscape" in the minds of her readers, "often vague and shadowy, . . . forming a quiet background, like the scenery of portraits in which the action of the lyric or the sonnet seem to lie."[78]

Symbolism in the Rossetti poems interests less than a quarter of her critics. Bell, an admirer of Rossetti's poems, finds "Autumn" (1858) particularly lovely and calls it highly "symbolical." It is also, he says, perhaps one of the most striking examples we possess of Christina's characteristic melancholy."[79] In it the speaker bemoans her loneliness and estrangement:

I dwell alone—I dwell alone, alone
  Whilst full my river flows down to the sea,
Gilded with flashing boats
  That bring no friend to me:
O love-songs, gurgling from a hundred throats,
  O love-pangs, let me be.

[337]

Aestheticism concerns a third of the Rossetti critics. Arthur Symons, for instance, finds "a peculiar charm" in the lyrics of *Sing-Song*. They are "as distinct and at the same time as immaterial and indescribable as a perfume. They are fresh with the freshness of dewy grass, or, in their glowing brightness, like a dewdrop turned by the sun into a prism."[80] Alice Law, in the *Westminster Review*, also comments on the unique beauty of Rossetti's poetry:

> Its beauty danced ever before me, but . . . it eluded capture . . . their seeming artless, yet aesthetic and finished perfections, all these combine to give the poems an air of elevated inaccessibility which renders critical approach difficult. . . . It is, I think, this power of reducing to poetic expression elements that are by nature, fleeting and volatile, which . . . lends such a characteristic air of charm and immateriality to Miss Rossetti's verse. Like some magic web, it seems woven of a substance so elusive, intangible, and of such an almost gossamer tenuity as defies handling, and constitutes at once the critic's ecstasy, wonder and despair.[81]

She points to "the artistic ardour which burns in such exquisite similes" as in the description of the two young maidens in "Goblin Market": "Laura stretched her gleaming neck / like a rush-imbedded swan." and "White and golden Lizzie stood / Like a lily in a flood."

The anonymous critic of the January 5, 1895, *Saturday Review* declares that in her modest way, Rossetti "awakens in us the sense of rarity and beauty" as very few poets do. We hear, he/she says, "the music of her verse afloat in the air, the very music of Ariel, and yet with all the intimacy of a perfume, the perfume of a flower; the soul of something living and beautiful, with its roots in the earth."[82]

Even more than figurative language, *form* occupies critics of the period. More than two-thirds of the reviewers discuss the simple diction and the musicality of Rossetti's verses. The *Saturday Re-*

view's January 1895, critic, for example, notes Rossetti's prefer-
ence for "the homeliest words, and the rhythms in which the art
consists in a seeming disregard of art,"[83] which is particularly evident in her ghost poems. This critic observes too that there are few
inversions, very little metaphor, and less dependence on the unusual in sound and color, all of which add to the simple style of
these poems.

Several critics comment on the simplicity of diction, not only in
Rossetti's ghost poems, but in her ballads as well. Benson says that
the poet, using old forms of austere simplicity, "laid a secure hand
on the precise medium required"[84] for the modern ballad, as
witness "Noble Sisters" (1860). The anonymous critic for the
Saturday Review of February 1896, praises Rossetti's "rare simplicity of diction and her mastery of simple metres" in the same
ballad. The form coincides with the meaning because "the simplicity of view and the deep sympathy with human passions give . . .
strength to these old [Scottish] Border ballads."[85]

Style is a consideration for the majority of critics reviewing Rossetti's work during this period. Almost inevitably they compare
the style of Christina Rossetti with that of her brother, Dante
Gabriel, noting the unadorned verses of the sister, the lavish ones
of her brother. In Symons's words:

> Unlike Dante Rossetti, whose noblest harmonics require the whole
> range of stops of the organ of verse, polysyllabic and consonanted
> harmonies, Christina Rossetti is most impressive in lines made up of
> short well-worn Saxon words; and while nearly all his finest efforts
> seem conscious, hers appear innocently unaware of their own beauty.[86]

Symons feels that the secret of this style is "its sincerity, leading to
the employment of homely words where homely words are
wanted, and always of natural and really expressive words."[87] Le
Gallienne in the *Academy* also compares Rossetti's lyrics with
those of Dante Gabriel and notes that Dante's "phrase is sumptuous with Latin, hers is ever simple with Saxon, her most haunting
rhyme-effects are in words of one syllable."[88]

All the reviewers who demonstrate an interest in Rossetti's nature poems discuss her simple diction, which yet manages to convey nature's glories. "Spring Quiet" (about May 1847) is often
cited as an exemplar:

> Gone were but the Winter,
>   Come were but the Spring,
> I would go to a covert
>   Where the birds sing;
>
> Where in the whitethorn
>   Singeth a thrush,
> And a robin sings
>   In the holly-bush.
>
> [103]

An anonymous critic of *Literary World* (Boston) in May 1876, praises the characteristic "sweetness and simplicity" of her verse and "its close kinship with and reflection of nature"[89] and admires the musical, simple lines of "A Green Cornfield" (before 1876):

> The earth was green, the sky was blue:
>   I saw and heard one sunny morn
> A skylark hang between the two
>   A singing speck above the corn;
>
> A stage below, in gay accord,
>   White butterflies danced on the wing,
> And still the singing skylark soared,
>   And silent sank and soared to sing.
>
> [389]

Most reviewers of the nature poems echo Symons's judgment:

Every poem almost leaves on the mind a sense of satisfaction, of rightness and fitness; we are not let to think of art, but we notice, almost unconsciously, that every little word seems to fit quite perfectly in its place, as if it could not possibly have come otherwise. This equable style, self-poised and instinctively select, seems by its simplicity and absence of emphasis, only faintly distinguished from the rhythms and tone of mere conversation. It has no italics, no waltz beats, nothing insistent, no unnecessary words; there is nothing of metre for metre's sake; absolutely no display. . . . While very few lines venture above a certain pitch, there is not a note which does not ring true.[90]

Perhaps a fifth of the critics call attention to the inconsistency of *meter* in some of Rossetti's poems, but most of them quickly add that they do not believe that it detracts from the work; in fact, they do not find the imperfect meter displeasing. As Alice Meynell states in calling attention to inconsistency in the meter of "The Prince's Progress" (1861–65)

> The poet has chosen to let the beats of her time fall punctually—and with full measure of time—now upon a syllable and now upon a rest within the *line;* so that the metre goes finely to time, like a nursery song for the rocking of a cradle. But then the succeeding stanza throws doubt upon the others. Read the poem which way you will, there is no assurance to the number of beats which she intended. . . . She has done a very serious service to English versification by using afresh this voice of poetry—the voice that sings in musical time.[91]

Rossetti's three-beat line in "The Prince's Progress," "Hark! the bride weepeth," is to Meynell an example of the poet's "strong, controlled, and leaping movement, that goes on living feet or living wings"—a contrast to the hasty meters used in the swifter lyrics of other poems.

Some 10 percent of the critics comment that Rossetti's sonnets lack technical precision; nevertheless they praise the metrical form of these verses. Edmund K. Chambers notes in the *Academy* that Rossetti's sonnets are "constructed with infinite care, with the same spirit of music in its rhythms, and with a subtle and audacious disposition of irregular accents to dispel all danger of monotony."[92] Symons, too, notices that the sonnets are not always technically correct, "yet whatever license appears is shown only in the arrangement of the rhymes, the art being otherwise always perfect, with . . . a stern and strong and sweet simplicity of phrasing."[93]

Benson finds fault with the metrical scheme: It is not strict enough; some lines have fewer syllables than others; and many of the poet's rhymes are vague. Yet, "whether it is that the directness and simplicity of the feeling overpowers all minute fastidiousness, or whether they are all part of the careful artlessness of the mood, is hard to determine."[94]

Symons says that Rossetti's spontaneity—as if "no word could possibly be otherwise"—is the main characteristic of her work. She does not attain this effect by limiting herself to certain religious topics or commonplace metrical arrangements, he observes. "Her metres are very frequently intricate, with much of ingenuity in them, much quaintness, peculiar turns and difficult monotones." Even in a deep mood, she will use a quaint conceit that startles us by its "profound and unthought-of naturalness."[95]

The Rossetti religious verses are the ones most often scrutinized for form and enthusiastically hailed by the critics. Lionel Johnson, writing for the *Academy* and speaking in general of the 300 sacred poems, finds

> all possible tones of feeling and thought. There are poems with a homely, carolling air about them, in their grace and sweetness, as though they were *(salva reverentia)*, the nursery songs of Heaven. There are poems, metrically and imaginatively marvellous, surging and sweeping forward with a splendor of movement to their victorious, their exultant close, as though they were the national hymns of Heaven.[96]

He claims that these pious poems help to "forward the ritual of Christian life."

A secular reviewer, the anonymous critic for the American edition of the January 22, 1898, issue of *Literature*, commends Rossetti's most popular religious poem of this period, part 3 of "Old and New Year Ditties" (1860) for many of the same qualities Johnson elaborates: "Not a word is out of place, not a cadence neglected, and the brief poem rises with a *crescendo* of passion. This is what all lyrical poets are called to do, but alas! how few are chosen' "[97]

The 1876 anonymous critic for the *Catholic World* notices a considerable difference between Rossetti's worldly poetry and her religious poetry, to the detriment of the former:

> In the one she warbles or sings, with often a flat and discordant note in her tones that now please and now jar; in the other she is an inspired prophetess or priestess chanting a sublime chant or giving voice to a world's sorrow and lament. In the latter all affection of word, or phrase, or rhythm disappears. The subjects sung are too great for such pettiness, and the song soars with them.[98]

The general run of Rossetti's poems "are nothing very wonderful, in whatever light we view them," because most of them do not show "any marked originality or individuality." Ah, but in the religious poems,

> Miss Rossetti has set up a little devotional shrine . . . where we find her on her knees, with a strong faith, a deep sense of spiritual needs, a feeling of the real littleness of the life passing around us, of the true greatness of what is to come after, a sense of the presence of the living God before whom she bows down her soul into the dust; and here she is another woman.[99]

For more than half of the critics writing for secular journals and
almost all of those writing for religious-oriented ones the ultimate
judgment of Rossetti's works appears to be based on their views of
the moral value of the verses. Even "Goblin Market," the long
narrative fantasy poem, is seen by several "secular" reviewers to
inculcate some moral lesson. Gosse, for example, perceives the
underlying theme of "Goblin Market" to be a "didactic one, and
nothing less than the sacrifice of self by a sister to recuperate a
sister's virtue."[100] A similar claim is made by James Benjamin
Kenyon in *Methodist Review:* There is a lesson to be gained from
the verses, as pointedly expressed in the closing lines:[101]

> 'For there is no friend like a sister
> In calm or stormy weather;
> To cheer one on the tedious way,
> To fetch one if one goes astray,
> To lift one if one totters down,
> To strengthen whilst one stands.'

[8]

A reviewer in the *Catholic World* issue of March 1867, writing
anonymously but known to be F. A. Rudd, sees a moral too, but
he calls it a questionable one: "Not 'resist the devil and he will flee
from you,' but 'cheat the devil, and he won't catch you.'" Rudd
asserts that some of Rossetti's poems "go inexcusably beyond the
bounds of that strict moral right, which every writer who hopes
ever to wield influence ought to keep steadily, and sacredly in
view."[102]

Concern with moral issues is seen also in the reviews of another
narrative fantasy poem, "The Prince's Progress." Gosse finds it
quite surprising that the "strange and unaccountable entity, 'Goblin Market' is more popular than 'The Prince's Progress,' where
the parable and the teachings are as clear as noonday." The moral
of "The Prince's Progress," he says, is that "no man can ignore the
influence of his tender years. Ultimately they will call to him and
draw him home, and it is a sacred call to be heeded. Only sorrow
awaits for those who delay too long."[103]

Alice Law thinks "most wonderful of all [The Prince's Progress"] is that unrivalled description of the 'life-less land,' typical of
the death and spiritual barrenness which follows the commission
of sin":[104]

> Off he set. The grass grew rare,
> A blight lurked in the darkening air,

The very moss grew hueless and spare,
    The last daisy stood all astunt;
Behind his back the soil lay bare,
    But barer in front.

[28]

Approximately a quarter of the critics commend the saintliness of Rossetti and her heroines. Kenyon claims that "in the poetry of Christina G. Rossetti may be clearly traced the austere beauty of a chaste nun-like spirit."[105] Others commend her heroines for their patient—and saintly—suffering. Alice Law finds a similarity between the women of these verses and the "long-tried Griseldas of ante-Renaissance type, the slow fading Isabella of Boccaccio, or the olive-wreathed flame-robed virgins of the Divine Comedy."[106]

But there is some disagreement about the character of Lizzie in "Goblin Market." To Law she is a saintly maid, but the *Catholic World*'s 1876 reviewer has a stricter standard of holiness. Although this critic declares that " 'Goblin Market' deserves a place beside 'The Pied Piper of Hamlin,' " Lizzie is no Joan of Arc, "merely a little girl struggling to prevent the little goblin-men from pressing their fatal fruit into her mouth! The statue is far too large for the pedestal."[107]

About a fifth of the critics discern and admire the "womanly" passion much in evidence in Rossetti's poetry. Among these is Amy Levy, writing in the February 1888 *Woman's World*, a magazine that offered its readers opinions on topical and literary matters in addition to items on fashion, cookery, and the home. "It is always her own voice—no echo—a woman's voice, curiously sweet, fantastically sad," with which Rossetti speaks, says Levy, who credits the poet with "a passionate woman's heart" combined with "an imagination deep and tender."

Levy asks her readers to consider the passion expressed in "Maude Claire" (1858), in which a stately heroine follows her faithless lover and his bride to the church, reproaching the man and taunting her successor. Only a woman could have written this poem, Levy says, because it expresses "a fervid human spirit; a passionate woman's heart; an imagination deep and tender; a fancy vivid and curious."[108]

What is the spirit of a woman's work? According to an anonymous critic for the general-interest magazine *Living Age* of April 1, 1899, women poets

as a rule, have a tendency to put more of what is called personal feeling into their writings than men; their creative mental life is less distinct from the outer practical one than is the case with men, as is evidenced from the fact that it is rare to find the spirit of a woman's work and her conduct in complete antagonism, while with men poets, painters, and artists of all kinds, the phenomenon is a frequent one. The reason is that a woman's personality dominates and permeates her character to a greater degree than does a man's; and, if we separate character from personality, of which it is but a part, and not the whole . . . we shall understand why characteristic tendencies and feelings appear more frequently and more pronouncedly in women's writings than in men's.[109]

To a quarter of her reviewers in the religious press and conservative press, Christina Rossetti offers more than a passionate woman's heart; she herself embodies their ideas of Christian womanhood. Says the anonymous critic for the *Saturday Review* of January 1895:

Content to be merely a woman, wise in limiting herself within somewhat narrow bounds, she possessed, in union with a profoundly emotional nature, a power of artistic self-restraint which no other woman who has written in verse has ever shown; and it is through this mastery over her own nature, this economy of her own resources, that she takes rank among poets rather than among poetesses.[110]

In February 1896, another anonymous *Saturday Review* critic praises Rossetti's unblemished personal life, which complements her religious verses and gives them even greater significance:

What a satisfaction it is to the lovers of her poetry to feel that there is nothing in her life to record unworthy of her high genius and her pure and noble work in verse! Her lovely verse was simply the expression of a lovely personality, exquisitely feminine, sweet and pure, good and worshipful. It is this, we think, that gives her devotional poems such unique charm and power.[111]

This reviewer praises above all "The Heart Knoweth Its Own Bitterness" (1857), a poem of "tragic depth" and earnestness":

> To give, to give, not to receive
>   I long to pour myself, my soul,
> Not to keep back or count or leave,
>   But king with king to give the whole.
> I long for one to stir my deep—
>   I have had enough of help and gift—

I long for one to search and sift
Myself, to take myself and keep.

. . . .
Not in this world of hope deferred,
   This world of perishable stuff:—
Eye hath not seen nor ear hath heard
   Nor heart conceived that full 'enough':
Here moans the separating sea,
   Here harvests fail, here breaks the heart:
   There God shall join and no man part,
I full of Christ and Christ of me.

                                          [192–93]

The October 1876, anonymous critic for the *Catholic World* lauds the womanly self-effacement evidenced in such religious poems as "Good Friday" (1862):[112]

Am I a stone, and not a sheep,
   That I can stand, O Christ,
      beneath Thy cross,
   To number drop by drop Thy
      Blood's slow loss
And yet not weep?

Not so those women loved
   Who with exceeding grief
      lamented Thee;
   Not so fallen Peter weeping
      bitterly;
Not so the thief was moved;

Not so the Sun and Moon
   Which hid their faces in a
      starless sky,
A horror of great darkness at broad
      noon—
   I, only I.

Yet give not o'er,
   But seek Thy sheep, true Shepherd
      of the flock;
   Greater than Moses, turn and look
      once more
And smite a rock.

                                          [234]

Rossetti's "passive feminity" and humility is praised not only by critics writing for religious publications, but also by those who prepare reviews for secular journals, albeit conservative ones. One such is Theodore Watts-Dunton, a poet, novelist, and critic who, in shedding theological light on the attitude of submission he finds in Rossetti's poems, manages to spark a controversy that continues into the twentieth century. As he writes in the *Athenaeum* of January 15, 1896, the "Christian idea" itself "is essentially feminine, and of this eminent quality Christina Rossetti's poetry is full." No male, ostensibly, can reflect the "Christian idea" as well:

> The history of literature shows no human develop so beautiful as the ideal Christian woman of our day. She is unique, indeed. Men of science tell us that among all the fossilized plants we find none of the lovely family of the rose, and in the same way we should search in vain through the entire human record for anything so beautiful as that kind of Christian lady to whom self-abnegation is not only the first of duties, but the first of joys.[113]

Smellie's review in *Wesleyan Methodist* goes even further, extolling Rossetti as one who "belongs to the order of the bond slaves of Jesus." He points out that other poets, such as Robert Browning and Alfred, Lord Tennyson, revered Jesus. But "perhaps because they were men and she was a woman, with a woman's directer vision and more childlike faith and warmer love, their testimony is not so simple and questioning as hers." To Smellie, Rossetti belongs "to the Church, catholic and eternal, which glories in the cross, and in Him who hastened to it for the joy of redeeming us." Is it "possible to repay Him with an affection too ardent or a consecration too complete?"[114] Rossetti's passion for Christ, Smellie says, pulsates through such verses as "Rejoice with Me" (before 1893):

> 'Little Lamb, who lost thee?'
>   'I myself, none other.'—
> 'Little Lamb, who found thee?'
>   'Jesus, Shepherd, Brother.
> Ah, Lord, what I cost thee!
>   Canst Thou still desire?'—
> 'Still Mine arms surround thee,
>   Still I lift thee higher,
>   Draw thee nigher.'

[223]

For the *Saturday Review* critic of January 1895, Rossetti "is not less conscious of human unworthiness than of the infinite charity of God; and in her passionate humility she prays for the lowest place in Paradise," for she feels even "that lowest place too high."[115] In fact "The Lowest Place" (1863) was the poem William Michael Rossetti chose as the inscription upon his sister's tombstone:

> Give me the lowest place: or if for me
> That lowest place too high, make
> one more low
> Where I may sit and see
> My God and Love Thee so.
>
> [237]

Christina Rossetti's place in literary history is assured, some critics maintain, because of her religious convictions. In February 1898, shortly after her death, W. Robertson Nicoll, a prominent critic, wrote in the illustrated London literary journal, the *Bookman*:

> She was, above other things, a Christian of the churchly type, and it is as an interpreter of Christianity, or rather of this phase of Christianity, that she will live. Those who are with her in her religious belief will, without hesitation, pronounce her the greatest of English religious poets.[116]

In February 1896, two years after Rossetti's death, the *Saturday Review* critic recalled "the love she had awakened in hearts of men and women, how much good she had done, . . . how genuinely and by how many she, not having been seen, was loved." Rossetti's verse "is tinged and coloured by her deep religious faith as a common cloud is glorified by the sunrise." She went through life "seeing the Invisible, and her view of life is not the less penetrating and true on this account—and when the judgment of the future is given, she will remain among the foremost poets of our time."[117]

We see that Christina Rossetti's contemporaries, critics of the 1862–99 period, were wont in a single review to sample a variety of her poems—narrative verse, nature lyrics, ghost poems, sonnets, and nursery rhymes in addition to the devotional poems. Most were content to provide a general overview of the Rossetti opus rather than a lengthy analysis of specific poems.

In their examination of a few poems in each category of the poet's work, these critics appeared eager to confirm what they held to be true; they sought, and found, evidence of Rossetti's cultural background, her loving relationship with family members, her sin-

cere devotion to contemporary social values and Christian principles. The poet's austere and ultra-respectable life-style was judged,
a priori and a posteriori, proof of a pious spirit.

About half of Rossetti's reviewers were writing for "Sunday
school presses" and sectarian or ecumenical journals, Protestant
and Catholic. Of the secular journals in which her works were
considered, most were of a decidedly conservative bent. The result
was a further predilection for judging the poems in terms of their
harmony with contemporary Christian social ethics. Themes,
form, characterization, even meter, were seen as successful if lent
to the task of leading readers along the path of right thinking and
acting. After all, was it not the purpose of literature "to instruct
and delight"?

"Delight" was apparently the more difficult measure for a Victorian critic to bring to Rossetti's works. Her fantasy poems, for
example, received a mixed response. Some critics who sought—
and failed—to discern meanings they felt lurking beneath the tales
of goblins and ghosts, called these poems disturbing. Others cared
little that meaning eluded them: These verses were to be ap-
preciated for their music, rich coloring, and vivid imagery.

Much of the interest in the fantasy verses was, in fact, a reflection of the critics' preoccupation with the Pre-Raphaelite movement, which strongly affected cultural tastes of the period. With
Rossetti's brother Dante Gabriel the Brotherhood's prime mover,
contemporary critics were bent on discerning Pre-Raphaelite ten-
denices in the fantasy poems' brilliant coloring, melancholy,
sepulchral scenery, and richness of detail. This was true of the
ghost poems as well.

Increased attention was paid to Rossetti's works upon her death
in 1894. The outpouring of eulogies and reminiscences about
Christina and her family were written mainly by critic-friends and
-acquaintances and by the religious press. In a form approaching
the testimonial, they bemoaned the loss of a pious voice in a skep-
tical world. There was lavish praise for a poet they were moved to
call the epitome of Christian womanhood.

William Michael also contributed, shortly after his sister's death,
a volume of *New Poems* (1896), which swelled the Rossetti opus.
The volume contained enough devotional poems to please traditional critics but also verses that communicated fears, bitterness,
and fierce passion—among them "Cousin Kate" (1859), "Sister
Maude" (1860), and "A Triad" (1856)—which had appeared in the

Goblin Market volume of 1862 but were withdrawn from subsequent editions. Though some reviewers speculated—albeit decorously—about what might have inspired the startling emotions revealed in these poems, evaluation and analysis of Rossetti's works—the wellsprings of its passionate intensity—had only just begun.

2

The Woman as Poet: Criticism, 1900–1939

We need, besides the shifting standard of contemporary taste, some fixed unit of judgment that never varies . . . and such a unit . . . can only be found in the final test of all art, the necessity of the moral idea. We must . . . control our standards—the one; the shifting standard of contemporary taste; the other the permanent standard of artistic justification, the presence of the moral idea. . . . The course of the highest thought of the time should be the course of its literature, the limit of the most delicate taste of the time, the limit of literary expression: whatever falls below that standard is a shortcoming, whatever exceeds it a violence.

Arthur Waugh, *Reticence in Literature*

The qualifications of a good critic are three. He must be an adept at experiencing . . . the state of mind relevant to the work of art he is judging. Secondly, he must be able to distinguish experiences from one another as regards their less superficial features. Thirdly, he must be a sound judge of values.

I. A. Richards, *Principles of Literary Criticism*

It is the very scope attempted by Mrs. Browning that prevents her from holding the place I would give to Christina Rossetti. So much of Mrs. Browning—her political ideas, her passion for reform, her scholarship—simply carries her into the sphere of the masculine poets, where she suffers by an unfair comparison.

Paul Elmer More, *Atlantic Monthly*

68

E ven before the first decade of the twentieth century was out, the controversy surrounding the name of Darwin had subsided. Evolution had invaded every branch of science and contributed to the development of such new ones as anthropology and sociology, entering into modern thought in such a way as to be almost indistinguishable as an independent factor. In literary criticism the "timeless standard" of old was giving way to a rather more subjective one, as witness Arthur Waugh's recognition of a "shifting standard of contemporary taste," though Waugh clings to a "permanent standard of artistic justification" by which the first must be measured.

Where Victorian critics were reticent in discussing the poet's biography as a means of illuminating her verse—though some hazarded the guess that emotions reflected in Rossetti's poetry had their source in her experience—we now find personal experience and subjective judgment recognized as vital factors in the production of a work of art. In fact, of the approximately one hundred and fifty critics who undertook an examination of Christina Rossetti's poetry in the period between 1900 and 1939, approximately half concerned themselves with the poetry's religiosity, moral lessons, and renunciation of earthly pleasures, while the other half were interested in relating her works to her biography.

The latter process was aided by the appearance in 1906 of William Michael Rossetti's "Memoir" introducing his edition of *The Poetical Works of Christina Rossetti.* Most eagerly pounced upon by reviewers was William Michael's revelation that his ascetic-appearing and otherworldly sister had had two formal suitors, James Collinson in her youth and Charles Bagot Cayley in her mature years, both of whom she had rejected for reasons of religious incompatibility. William Michael hinted that he was withholding still more from public view.

One finds in the first decades of the new century, too, a growing awareness of the-female-as-writer, a type of recognition that women of today may find unwelcome but that conferred a form of status upon its recipients and led to extended comparisons with sister littérateurs, of whom there were more in the Victorian period than in the entire literary history of England.

This period is also marked by the first outcroppings of psychocriticism, influenced by Freud's revolutionary attempts to understand human behavior, not only through the intellect, but though the psyche as well, and his thesis that writers disguise their egoistic daydreams in the presentation of their fantasies. In these years, too, the complementary psychology of Carl Jung was introduced, offering a whole new approach to literature in its search for archetypal myths—preconscious cultural forces at the roots of the mind's working.

Of course Freudian and Jungian theories did not change literary criticism all at once. Many of the critics in the first three decades of the twentieth century reevaluated such Victorian ideals as reticence and modesty and decided to set their standards by them. Still others, while rebelling against the conventions of literary criticism, were tentative in their embrace of new matter.

There was an increasing number of critical reviews of Rossetti's works by Americans—now more than a third of the total—in the first decades of the twentieth century, after a singular paucity in the first period. Leading American publishers and university presses undertook critical studies of the poet. American critics contributed articles about Rossetti to United States periodicals. And articles and books about Rossetti, originally published in England, were being reprinted simultaneously or a few years later in American books and journals. However, fewer religious journals undertook to review the poet's work in this era.

A few of Rossetti's reviewers in the early twentieth century approach the poet's sources of inspiration almost as gingerly as did the run of critics in the nineteenth. Yet, even while treading softly, a reviewer such as A. J. Green-Armytage can capture a new feeling about the poet and her works. The *Monna Innominata* sonnets (1882), he writes in *Maids of Honour* (1906),

> seem so autobiographical as to be almost sacred. We feel while reading them, as probably many have felt while reading the "Browning Love Letters," as if they ought not to be in our possession,—that they are too private for the rude and prying eyes of the public. And yet, is not all the truest poetry the outcome of personal experience. . . ? He who has not known sorrow can never appeal to a broken heart; he who realises nothing of the joys of life, its wealth of beauty and its vastness of possibility, can never quicken another soul into enthusiasm, or make our pulses thrill with the knowledge that it is good for us to be here.[1]

But by the third decade of the century, fully a quarter of Rossetti's critics were "prying" into those very hopes, fears, passions, and tensions for the light they might shed on the poet's biography or were training a similar psychological lens on the known or speculated-about facts of the poet's life for the insights they might yield into the works themselves. Among the incidents of Rossetti's life to which most critics turned is her rejection of the suitors Collinson and Cayley.

The author of *Christina Rossetti and Her Poetry* (1930), for example, finds evidence that Rossetti renounced her two suitors because she "was fearful lest she should love the creature more than the Creator."[2] Furthermore, says Edith Birkhead, no doubt influenced by the revelations in William Michael Rossetti's "Memoirs," it was the renunciation of James Collinson that affected the poet more deeply. Virginia Moore, writing in the *Yale Review* of December 1930, sees Rossetti's rejection of her suitors as a matter of giving in to still other fears. The poet wished to love and be loved: "But deeper than love was religion, and deeper than religion was fear—fear at the roots of her, fear of the known, fear of the unknown, fear of losing the safety of her mother, fear of tempting the terrible wrath of God."[3] Although the poet gave religious incompatibility as the reason for her refusal to marry Cayley and Collinson, Moore asserts, it was merely an excuse to herself and the world.

For the pseudonymous Frances Winwar (Mrs. Frances Grebanier), author of *Poor Splendid Wings: The Rossettis and Their Circle* (1933), Rossetti broke her engagement to Collinson simply upon realizing that she did not love him. "Why that gloom at the height of her happiness?" Winwar asks, considering it odd that at the very time the poet loved most and seemed most happy, she was writing melancholy poems about young girls dying before their marriages. Perhaps "all those dead girls were dead selves, selves that she had wished dead, rather than in love unworthily."[4] Winwar notes that the poem "When I am Dead, My Dearest" (1848) was written during this "happy" betrothal time.

It was not Collinson's fault that his personality was timid and weak, hence no match for that of her beloved brother Gabriel, says Winwar. And the poet, upon marrying, would have had to leave her beloved mother, a thought not to be endured. "The fledgling dove she had brought out to see the sun shrank back and was afraid. The tremulous wings folded closer to the nest."[5]

For Violet Hunt, friend of the Rossetti family and biographer of Lucy Brown Rossetti, wife of William Michael, the issue is not Collinson's weakness but his place in a dread secret kept by the poet. Hunt asserts in *The Wife of Rossetti* (1932) that the lines in "Goblin Market"—"For there's no love like a sister's . . ."—refer to Rossetti's elder unattractive, pious sister Maria who attempted to play the savior to sullied women. She would read to the surly

"The Girlhood of Mary Virgin" by Dante Gabriel Rossetti, 1848–1849. Frances, Christina, and William Michael Rossetti were the models. Rossetti's first famous painting.

outcasts who languished in institutions in Highgate and in Portobello Road, determined to rescue them from their sinful lives. Hunt claims it was Maria, "the kind, sonsy creature," who, for a week, "crouched on the mat by the house door and saved her sister from the horrors of an elopement with a man (Collinson) who belonged to another." This is what caused "the terrible pain" of guilt and remorse in so many of Rossetti's poems, a secret "so dreadful then to the lay mind that no one had the moral hardihood to read between the lines."[6]

Eudora Zaidee Green claims in the March 1936, number 62 of the *English Review*—a journal of current affairs and literature—that self-centeredness and playacting determined the course of Christina Rossetti's life and art. As an adolescent, Green observes, the poet wrote conventional poems of blighted romance, and even in her devotional poems of this period she used merely the traditional symbols of religion: lilies, doves, lambs, and cherubim. However, from the time that her brother Dante Gabriel used Christina as a model for the Virgin in his painting *The Girlhood of Mary Virgin*, we find her "figuratively holding a lily in her hand, and we see her continue to clutch this flower of faith throughout the greater part of her life." She was playacting the role of Virgin, Green says, "to measure up to her brother's famous painting, to be what the young men of the Pre-Raphaelite Brotherhood, in their youth, would have her be." Had not Rossetti been in love with her griefs, and had she "not chosen to play the role of saint," she could have aroused by her intensely passionate nature "a less fickle nature than Collinson's, and even more remote nature than Cayley's."[7]

Eleanor Walter Thomas, author of *Christina Georgina Rossetti* (1931), finds not a hint of insincerity in the poet's proclamations of faith. While Rossetti was considering marriage, Thomas notes, she was writing poems of earthly and spiritual love, illustrating an emotional conflict between "the love of the human and the perishable and the Divine and eternal." In poem after poem, she stresses "the greatness of Christ's love, His suffering for man, His supreme sacrifice," and always wonders "can she give Him the all that He requires?"[8] This conflict manifests itself in "Despised and Rejected" (1864) in which Christ knocks at a door which will not open to Him:

> But all night long that voice spake urgently,
> 'Open to Me.'
> Still harping in mine ears:

'Rise, let Me in.'
Pleading with tears:
'Open to Me, that I may come to thee.'
While the dew dropped, while the dark hours were cold:
'My Feet bleed, see My Face,
See My Hands bleed that bring thee grace,
My Heart doth bleed for thee,—
Open to Me."

So till the break of day:
Then died away
That voice, in silence as of sorrow;
Then footsteps echoing like a sigh
Passed me by,
Lingering footsteps slow to pass.
On the morrow
I saw upon the grass
Each footprint marked in blood, and on my door
The mark of blood for evermore.[9]

Percy H. Osmond, author of the *The Mystical Poets of the English Church* (1919), commenting on "Now They Desire" (1856)—one of the verses withheld by Rossetti but published after her death by William Michael—considers that it has "the authentic accent of a mystical soul," but adds, echoing Green: "This erotic type of the mystical consciousness has its temptations to become merely self-regarding":

There is a Love which fills desire
    And can our love require:
Like fire it draws our lesser fire,
    Like greater light our light:
For it we agonize in strife,
    We yearn, we famish thus—
Lo, in the far-off land of life
    Doth it not yearn for us?

[187]

Osmond notes that Rossetti herself recognized "this danger" in "Take Care of Him" (before 1882), and he quotes Swinburne as styling the poem " 'a shrine of holiest-hearted song' ":[10]

'Thou whom I love, for whom I died,
    Lovest thou Me, My bride?'—
Low on my knees I love Thee, Lord,

Believed in and adored.
. . . .
'In Me thou lovest Me: I call
    Thee to love Me in all.'—
Brim full my heart, dear Lord, that so
    My love may overflow.

. . . .
'Love me in sinners and in saints,
    In each who needs or faints,'—
Lord, I will love Thee as I can
    In every brother man.

[257]

Some 20 percent of the critics in this era remark the saintliness of
the poet herself, though appreciably fewer than in an earlier time.
When it comes to characterizing its effect on Rossetti's works,
they—quite unlike those earlier critics—may offer a disdainful
comment or two. For Eugene Mason, author of *A Book of Preferences in Literature* (1915), the two keynotes of Rossetti's character
were "poetess and saint." To be either a saint or poet is a mark of
distinction, he says, but Rossetti had the honor of being both. He
finds it ironic, however, that while an ordinary man faces the
future cheerfully, "this Anglican saint almost feared to pass that
country where in truth she had always dwelt."[11]

Virginia Moore in her *Yale Review* essay of 1930 ranks Rossetti
with "that unworldly race of fanatics, saints, dire prophets and
pure mystics who subsist alternately on fear and faith, and whose
natural garb is a harsh hair shirt."[12]

Sister M. Madeleva, author of *Chaucer's Nuns and Other Essays*
(1925), praises the "patient sweetness" of Rossetti's devotional
poems but calls the poet's maintenance of a single attitude "almost
a disease; her homesickness for heaven is near to hypochondria."
To Rossetti, this Catholic religious says, earth was a place of exile,
and, remembering Jerusalem, she wrote mostly mournful songs.
"She was a poet of the Passion rather than of the Resurrection."[13]

But Osbert Burdett, author of *The Beardsley Period* (1925), claims
that "the life and poetry of Christina Rossetti were the fit reflection of each other. . . . Her seclusion was proper to a contemplative
mystic. She was a poet and a saint, one of those whom the Church
of England has placed its soul in peril by neglecting."[14]

Virginia Woolf's *The Second Common Reader* (1932) finds gig-
gles and grunts to be as characteristic of Rossetti as her saintly
austerity:

Your God was a harsh God, your heavenly crown was set with thorns. No sooner have you feasted on beauty with your eyes than your mind tells you that beauty is vain and beauty passes. Death, oblivion, and rest lap round your songs with their dark wave. And then incongruously, a sound of scurrying laughter is heard. There is the patter of animals' feet and the odd gutteral notes of rooks and the snufflings of obtuse furry animals grunting and nosing. For you were not a pure saint by any means. You pulled legs; you tweaked noses. You were at war with all humbug and pretense. Modest as you were, still you were drastic, sure of your gift, convinced of your vision. A firm hand pruned your lines; a sharp ear tested their music. Nothing soft, otiose, irrelevant cumbered your pages. In a word, you were at artist.[15]

More than the generalized notion of saintliness, it is the themes of renunciation and of love entwined with death that interest reviewers of this period—fully half of those who address her works. Thomas comments, for instance, that the theme of love renounced on earth to be avowed anew in the afterlife—the stuff of "The Convent Threshold" (1858)—is itself autobiographically inspired. Here a novice is writing to the man with whom she has sinned, "a pleasant sin" and from whom she has been separated by her father and her brother. Her lover remains enthralled by earthly pleasures, and she now entreats him to repent his sins and climb with her the "kindled stair" to heaven;

> My lily feet are soiled with mud,
> With scarlet mud which tells a tale
> Of hope that was, of guilt that was,
> Of love that shall not yet avail;
> . . . .
> I seek the sea of glass and fire
> To wash the spot, to burn the snare;
> Lo, stairs are meant to lift us higher
> Mount with me, mount the kindled stair.

[340]

Thomas does not share the opinion of Dante Gabriel, who had called the poem "a very splendid piece of feminine asceticism." To the contrary, she says, the passion of the noviate "is surely not altogether ascetic because in one mood she does not regret the past and even shrinks from the future":[16]

> How long must stretch those years and years?
>
> I turn from you my cheeks and eyes,

My hair which you shall see no more—
Alas for joy that went before,
For joy that dies, for love that dies!

[341]

Fredegond Shove, author of *Christina Rossetti: A Study* (1931), asserts that some of Rossetti's poems expose "the soul's own inmost drama; its fears, its penitence, its hopes, its anguish, dryness and desolation." They reveal that "Christina Rossetti's peace of mind was not cheaply bought and her religious life was, especially in youth, one long interior struggle towards harmony, one unceasing and relentlessly exhausting fight against self."[17] A poem like "The Heart Knoweth Its Own Bitterness" (1857), Shove claims, shows the poet expressing the sincere but fiery ardors of a young Saint Teresa:

When all the over-work of life
 Is finished once, and fast asleep
We swerve no more beneath the knife
 But taste that silence cool and deep;
Forgetful of the highways rough,
 Forgetful of the thorny scourge,
 Forgetful of the tossing surge,
Then shall we find it is enough?

[192]

Joseph J. Reilly, writing in *America*—"A Catholic Review of the Week"—on February 14, 1931, states that Rossetti's renunciation of earthly love "strengthened her religious feeling by ennobling her passion and making her faith more intense and sensitively alert to the countless spiritual needs of life." One understands why her renunciation is sometimes accompanied by tears: "She lifts up her eyes, but her heart, alas, seems divided." Reilly offers as a telling example of this thesis, "Dost Thou Not Care?" (1864):

I love and love not: Lord, it breaks my heart
 To love and not to love.
Thou veiled within Thy glory, gone apart
 Into Thy shrine which is above,
Dost Thou not love me, Lord, or care
 For this mine ill?—
'I love thee here or there,
 I will accept thy broken heart—
  lie still.'

[242–3]

To Reilly the poet's life is a *"via dolorosa"* as she makes her way "struggling, panting up to God." Her verse was often sorrowful," he says, "but it was never morbid after she remembered the promise of abiding peace beyond the strife, of eternal morning beyond the shadows," and always with a deep humility, as witness "Of Him That Was Ready to Perish" (before 1882):[18]

> Lord I am waiting, weeping, watching for Thee:
>   My youth and hope lie by me buried and dead,
>   My wandering love hath not where to lay its head
>   Except Thou say "Come to Me."
>
> [253]

In a later work, *Dear Prue's Husband and Other People* (1932), Reilly claims that Rossetti's poetry "provided an outlet for the emotions and spiritual yearnings of this sensitive, delicately conscienced woman whose ardent nature had made its great renunciation and crowned its high desires not with bridal lilies but with thorns."[19]

Geoffrey W. Rossetti, a family member, sees in such early works as "Three Nuns" (1849–50) something similar: a "sense of otherworldliness, of sin on earth contrasted to the purity of heaven," and recommends to readers of the *Criterion* of October 10, 1930, the third section of the poem:

> Thou world from which I am come out,
>   Keep all thy gems and gold;
> Keep thy delights and precious things,
>   Thou that art waxing old.
> My heart shall beat with a new life
>   When thine is dead and cold;
> When thou dost fear I shall be bold.
>
> When Earth shall pass away with all
>   Her pride and pomp of sin,
> The City builded without hands
>   Shall safely shut me in.
> All the rest is but vanity
>   Which others strive to win:
> Where their hopes end my joys begin.
>
> [15]

As to the poet's enormous interest in death and pain evinced in later works, Rossetti suggests that this was the result of "religious melancholy" coupled with the effects "of the prolonged ill-health and troubles of later life"—some of it perhaps produced by a "semi-pathological condition of the body."[20]

Mary F. Sandars attributes Rossetti's preoccupation with death to her continual ill health and vivid imagination. The result, says Sandars, in *The Life of Christina Rossetti* (1930), was that the mysterious realm of the afterlife was always on her mind: "She was stern in her beliefs; the present life was a time of prohibition, which mis-spent, condemned the soul to an eternal hell." "The Martyr" (1846), a poem written in the poet's adolescence, concerns a young girl about to be burned at the stake for her beliefs. A loss of faith at the last moment of her life would bar the doors of heaven against her forever":[21]

> See, the sun hath risen—
> Lead her from the prison;
> She is young and tender,—lead her
> tenderly:
> May no fear subdue her,
> Lest the saints be fewer—
> Lest her place in heaven be lost
> eternally.
>
> [91]

Frank Jewett Mather, Jr., writing on "The Rossettis" for the New York-based *Bookman* of April 1919, claims that the love sonnets of renunciation in the *Monna Innominata* sequence "are stripped down to sheer feeling" and wonders "with what feelings the learned old bachelor Charles Cayley read it." Sonnet 11, Mather declares, reflects the intensity of the speaker's emotions:

> Many in aftertimes will say of you
> 'He loved her'—while of me what
> will they say?
> Not that I loved you more than
> just in play,
> For fashion's sake as idle women do.
> Even let them prate; who know not
> what we knew
> Of love and parting in exceeding
> pain,
> Of parting hopeless here to meet
> again,
> Hopeless on earth, and heaven is
> out of view,

But by my heart of love laid bare to
    you,
  My love that you can make not
      void nor vain,
Love that foregoes you but to claim
    anew
Beyond this passage of the gate of
    death,
  I charge you at the Judgment
      make it plain
My love of you was life and not a
    breath.

                                            [62]

The exquisiteness of the work's poetic value Mather does not deny,
but "With the life renouncing passion of Christina Rossetti," he
says, "I have the smallest sympathy."[22]

Shove contends too that it is possible to admire Rossetti's poetry
"whilst remaining chill to her passionate Christianity." Alas, he
comments, "I think that all such admirers of Christina Rossetti's
work are bound to lose more than half of her message not only of
the sense but of the full beauty and rhythmic life in it because the
"melodious lines run ever parallel to the harmony in the thought,
keeping tune and time with her pleasant Christian hope."[23] For
him, "Easter Day" (before 1886) is an exemplar:

Words cannot utter
    Christ His returning:
Mankind, keep jubilee,
    Strip off your mourning,
Crown you with garlands,
    Set your lamps burning.

Speech is left speechless;
    Set you to singing,
Fling your hearts open wide,
    Set your bells ringing:
Christ the Chief Reaper
    Comes, His sheaf bringing.

Earth wakes her song-birds,
    Puts on her flowers,
Leads out her lambkins,
    Builds up her bowers:

> This is man's spousal day,
> Christ's day and ours.

> [168]

Shove points out that Rossetti's love for God "was oftener thought of in the glorious second Person of the Trinity than in either the first or the third" and was "the heart-pulse and main spring of her whole poetic output."[24] She was constantly preoccupied by "Our blessed Lord's Passion, His agony on the Cross," and her religious life was "rooted on Calvary." Sister Madeleva, we remember, said as much, though less admiringly than Shove.

Anna Kimball Tuell, author of *A Victorian at Bay* (1932), claims that she has trouble in approaching the religious poetry of Christina Rossetti: Religious poetry "is always daring. . . . So suspicious are we of cant in what purports to be a religious voice that the religious lyric must endure a more rigorous test than another." Rossetti's religious poems are her best, Tuell says, yet "only with reluctance will we allow it to have a genuine accent."[25]

Doctrinal matters are sometimes invoked in discussing the theme of renunciation in the devotional poems. In *Memories and Impressions* (1911), Ford Madox Hueffer, novelist, essayist, and critic, comments as follows on Rossetti's belief on her deathbed that her soul would be damned because of her sins:

> It was a terrible thought to go down to Death with, and it has always seemed to me to be a condemnation of Christianity that it should have let such a fate harass such a woman, just as perhaps it is one of the greatest testimonies to the powers of discipline of Christianity that it should have trained up such a woman to such a life of abnegation, of splendid literary expression, and of meticulous attention to duty.

By blood and by nature, Hueffer adds, Rossetti should have been a Catholic, but by upbringing and all the influence around her, she was forced to be a Protestant. "Under the influence of a wise confessor the morbidities of her self-abnegation would have been checked."[26]

Margaret Mackenzie, writing about Rossetti for the January 1932, issue of *Thought: Fordham University Quarterly,* published by the Jesuit-run institution in New York, states that

> Fate had robbed her of her Catholic inheritance and imprisoned her in the falsity of the English Church. She was too true a person to be at

ease there and could only cling to what was real in it. The doctrines, torn from Catholicism, that it gave her were without roots and could not blossom in her soul.[27]

The Pre-Raphaelite influences in literature and art, strong in the latter part of the nineteenth century, had begun to wane in the early years of the twentieth. Yet the search for Pre-Raphaelite influences in Rossetti's poetry is still carried on by her critics. For example, Dorothy Margaret Stuart, author of *Christina Rossetti* (1930), names several poems—"The Prince's Progress" (1861–65), "Goblin Market" (1859), "Convent Threshold" (1858), "An Apple Gathering" (1857), and "Cousin Kate" (1859), among others—in the Pre-Raphaelite category. These poems, Stuart contends, have certain features in common: "the vividness, almost the violence, of their colour-values, their high, almost febrile emotional tension; their artificiality, which seldom lapses into affection yet is far removed from the unpremeditated grace of her finest lyrics." Despite the Pre-Raphaelite influence in many of Rossetti's poems, "she is not an imitator, rather an innovator," says Stuart, who doubts these poems would have been different had there been no such brotherhood and finds it difficult to determine whether Rossetti helped the movement or the movement helped her. The poems "most intimately hers," according to Stuart, "are the least Pre-Raphaelite in complexion."[28]

Eleanor Thomas also notes the Pre-Raphaelite touches in "Goblin Market": "the riotous description of the fruit, its odors, the fresh bloom upon it so pleasant to the touch, is joined with the suggestion of rich color or sheen; purple and golden flags, blue-veined stone, dew-pearly night."[29]

About a third of the critics in this period read several of Rossetti's poems allegorically or symbolically. Eleanor Thomas, for example, asserts that the poet often employs the familiar comparisons of life to a journey, a voyage, a perilous sea in remote realms of sleep or death:

> The greater number of Rossetti's allegorical poems may be grouped by theme: allegories of life moving toward death, of life distracted by worldly pleasure, of life postponing its highest good because of indifference or folly, or life spent in the unresting search after the unattainable; allegories of love dying, frustrated, or renounced, and of the shutting out of joy; and allegories of the Christian life.[30]

One such poem, Thomas states, is "Sleep at Sea" (1853), an allegory of life at sea, its passengers unconcerned about where they are or whether heading in the wrong direction:

> Sound the deep waters:—
>   Who shall sound that deep?—
> Too short the plummet,
>   And the watchmen sleep.
> Some dream of effort
>   Up a toilsome steep;
> Some dream of pasture grounds
>   For harmless sheep.
>
> . . . .
>
> So dream the sleepers,
>   Each man in his place;
> The lightning shows the smile
>   Upon each face;
> The ship is driving,—driving,—
>   It drives apace:
> And sleepers smile, and spirits
>   Bewail their case.
>
> [154–55]

Louis Cazamian, author of *A History of English Literature: Modern Times* (1927), believes that the most substantial of Rossetti's poems, such as "Goblin Market," are

allegories in which we watch a curiously imaginative mind at work, weaving out of an exclusively psychological sensuality an exuberance of description, and toning down the passionate element to innocent caresses, whilst the conscience, secretly astir, is preoccupied by a kind of gracious symbolism.

The charm and gay spirit that permeates this airy fantasy, he says, "serve to conceal a theme of graver import: the dread of sensual folly, and the security inherent in a doctrine of sacrifice and renunciation."[31]

Eugene Mason claims that "Goblin Market" is really a "parable of redemption through a sister's love." Behind the "muffler" of this delightful fantasy, "we seem to spy a beard."[32]

Thomas remarks of the same poem that Rossetti's sensuous imagination is peculiarly stimulated by fruit: "The extreme lusciousness of the fruit suggests the allurement of sin, and there is a touch of the uncanny and sinister as in other romantic bowers of bliss."[33]

Oliver Elton, author of *A Survey of English Literature 1830–1880*, volume 2 (1920), rejects such a suggestion: "Goblin Market" is a good fairy tale, with a latent note of mischief, sadism, and pain, he asserts—one that "has no moral, but there is no reason in it." It *plays* with spiritual ideas "in such a way as to get home; with the ideas of temptation, entrapment by evil, and sacrifice and rescue. Still it stops short of symbol." His final judgment: It "is a small masterpiece, and has no fellow."[34]

Frank Jewett Mather, Jr., claims that " 'Goblin Market' mingles the symbolic, quaint, graphic, and tender into a fashion elsewhere unequaled."[35]

Dorothy Margaret Stuart finds allegorical aspects in "The Prince's Progress" a long narrative poem that, like "Goblin Market," contains elements of fantasy. It is about a roving Prince, "strong of limb, if of purpose weak"—to Stuart, a representation of "Everyman." The Prince is tempted by a siren in the form of a milkmaid, with whom he dallies for a whole long summer day and night. When he continues on his journey, the landscape changes from daisied meadow to "A lifeless land, a loveless land, / Without lair or nest on either hand, / Only scorpions jerked in the sand, / Black as black iron or dusty pale."

He seeks rest in a glowing cavern, where "an old, old mortal cramped and double" is stirring a cauldron over a livid flame, whose contents contain an elixir of life, missing only one ingredient. It is eventually supplied by the finger of this aged man as he dies at his task. Stuart claims that "This cavern interlude may be intended to typify the innate tendency of poor Everyman to find specious pretexts for his wanderings from the hard and steep path."

When the Prince comes at last to the palace of his betrothed, who had patiently watched and waited for him, he is "Too late for love, too late for joy, . . . The Bride not seen to be seen no more / Save of Bridegroom Death." Stuart ventures that the golden virgin whom the Prince fails to marry may represent "truth, maybe, or Righteousness, or Salvation, or the Grace of God," yet finds the "allegorical element dulls the pleasure and deflects the interest of the reader."[36]

But Geoffrey Rossetti can find no allegory here. Although there is an *illusion* of the fantastic and the unreal in "The Prince's Progress," he writes, "it is very near in time and space, for the weakness of the Prince is very human weakness."[37]

Edith Birkhead calls "Sleep at Sea" a symbolic poem that seems "to shadow forth in symbol Rossetti's fear lest those who dream of earthly happiness may fail to hear the call of the spirit world":[38]

> 'Wake,' call the spirits:
>   But to heedless ears;
> They have forgotten sorrows
>   And hopes and fears;
> They have forgotten perils
>   And smiles and tears;
> Their dream has held them long,
>   Long years and years.
>
> . . . .
> No voice to call the sleepers,
>   No hand to raise:
> They sleep to death in dreaming
>   Of length of days
> Vanity of vanities,
>   The Preacher says:
> Vanity is the end
>   Of all their ways.
>
> [155–56]

Birkhead sees symbolism, too, in "A Ballad of Boding" (before 1882), in which three "barges of manifold adorning" are symbolic of three ways of life. The first, with its sails like fire, its choristers who breathe into flutes and finger soft guitars, is a love ship: "The first barge showed for figure-head a / Love with wings." The second, which "showed for figurehead a Work with strings," is chosen by the worldly wise who desire power, wealth, and knowledge: "Wider-visioned, graver, / More distance of purpose, more sustained of will." The third has no choir, no feast, no prizes; those on board "toiled in rowing . . . laboured at the oar handsore." But it alone represents the "ark of the Christian faith," Birkhead says, "whose purity and love are symbolized by the lily and the rose, resists the wiles of the devil, and, rescued by the Saviour, steers into the splendour of the sky." Birkhead believes that this poem is a representation of Rossetti's life. When the poet's first love-ship foundered, she was afraid to sail forth again in so fragile a bark. "She chose the barge with sackcloth for its sail."[39]

Eleanor Thomas comments that a succession of images that reflect the poet's moods strengthen the meaning of Rossetti's lyrics.[40] The images in "A Birthday" (1857), for example, express rapture—while the sonnet "Cobwebs" (1855) expresses the opposite mood of apathy and lifelessness—

> It is a land with neither night nor
>   day,
>   Nor heat nor cold, nor any wind
>   nor rain,
>   Nor hills nor valleys: but one
>   even plain
> Stretches through long unbroken
>   miles away.
> While through the sluggish air a
>   twilight grey
>   Broodeth: no moons or seasons
>   wax and wane,
>   No ebb and flow are there along
>   the main,
> No bud-time, no leaf-falling, there
>   for aye:—
> No ripple on the sea, no shifting
>   sand
>   No beat of wings to stir the
>   stagnant air:
> No pulse of life through all the
>   loveless land
> And loveless sea; no trace of days
>   before,
>   No guarded home, no toil-worn
>   resting-place,
> No future hope, no fear for ever-
>   more.

[317–18]

In Rossetti's religious poems, Thomas points out, the poet uses conventional symbols such as the harp, the crown, the lily, the rose, the dove, the lamb, the Bridegroom and His bride. In her nature poems she refers to common things that acquire significance according to the poet's mood: The cankered apple, the abandoned nest of eggs, the trapped robin trouble her in her daily walk; flowers, such as those found in English gardens, particularly the heliotrope, the crocus, the passion flower, the poppy, and the blossoms of peach and apple, gladden her.[41] An example is "Balm in Gilead" (before 1886):

> Heartsease I found where Love-
>   lies-bleeding
>   Empurpled all the ground:
> Whatever flower I missed unheeding,
> Heartsease I found.
>   Yet still my garden mound
> Stood sore in need of watering, weeding,
>   And binding growths unbound.
>
> Ah when shades fell, to light succeeding,
>   I scarcely dared look round:
> 'Love-lies-bleeding' was all my pleading:
>   Heartsease I found.
>
> [134]

A few critics examine Rossetti's poems for the archetypical images and myths on which they may be based. These reviewers approach her works seeking images and symbols that stress the racial origins of personality, a Jungian postulate. George Lowther, a critic for the November 1913 *Contemporary Review*, a journal of literary criticism, theology, history, and social issues, detects in Rossetti's works

> a double sense of sojourning and of homeliness, which is found only in religious poetry. It dates from the powerful symbol of the wilderness and the Land of Promise, which has underlain all Christian ideas of earth and heaven, but its origin is older yet. It arose in that elementary strife in the heart of man, coeval with his birth, the inward strife between his restlessness and his craving for peace. Whatever heaven might mean for him, it meant a homely place, where he would be surrounded by all loved, familiar things. Whatever perfections of beauty and abundance it might have, it would be an abiding city, a home for the weary dwellers in tents.[42]

An instance of this "homeliness," he says, is found in the poem "Up-hill" (1858):

> Shall I find comfort, travel-sore and
>   weak?
>   Of labour you shall find the sum.
> Will there be beds for me and all
>   who seek?
>   Yea, beds for all who come.
>
> [330]

Eleanor Thomas, too, points out the archetypal images and the presence of the quest-myth, a familiar theme in the literature of all peoples, in "Up-hill" and its companion piece, "Amor Mundi" (1865):

> 'Oh where are you going with your
>   love-locks flowing,
>   On the west wind blowing along
>   this valley track?'
> 'The downhill path is easy, come
>   with me and it please ye,
>   We shall escape the uphill by
>   never turning back."
>
> . . . .
>
> 'Turn again, O my sweetest,—turn
>   again, false and fleetest:
>   This beaten way thou beatest, I
>   fear, is hell's own track.'
> 'Nay, too steep for hill mounting;
>   nay, too late for cost counting:
>   This downhill path is easy, but
>   there's no turning back.'
>
> [374–75]

She notes that "the familiar comparison of life to a journey or aspiration after an ideal to the pursuit of an ever eluding phantom are the bases of some of Christina's finest poems."[43] The two poems are a study in contrasts, says Thomas. "Up-hill" illustrates the difficulty of the ascent to Heaven, while "Amor Mundi" illustrates the ease of the descent to the path of folly, which leads to hell.

Among the several critics interested in the beauty evoked in Rossetti's poems is Joseph Reilly in *Dear Prue's Husband and Other People.* "Christina Rossetti's sense of life's vanities and her other-worldliness did not blind her to the beauties all about her," he avers. Despite her sense of the impermanence of all worldly things, the beauty of "a bed of violets, a nesting lark, a rolling moon, roses unveiled to the sun, rivers seeking the sea, the graying twilight, the twitter of birds about the eaves, autumn fruits, and winter with its 'frostful blast' all bore in upon her consciousness."[44] For Claude C. H. Williamson, author of *Writers of Three Centuries, 1789–1914,* "to browse amongst [Rossetti's] poems is like wandering in the meadows in May."[45]

Desmond Lionel Morse-Boycott, a contributor to *Lead, Kindly*

Light (1933), a study of the saints of the Oxford Movement, finds it ironic that Rossetti, "whose artistic nature . . . loved beauty, who created beauty and could not help creating beauty all her life, went so far as to say that beauty in a woman is of no importance at all, because in the end she must die.[46] The poet's expression of this is contained in "Beauty Is Vain" (1864):

> While roses are so red,
> While lilies are so white,
> Shall a woman exalt her face
> Because it gives delight?
> She's not so sweet as a rose,
> A lily's straighter than she,
> And if she were as red or white
> She'd be but one of three.
>
> Whether she flush in love's summer
> Or in its winter grow pale,
> Whether she flaunt her beauty
> Or hide it away in a veil,
> Be she red or white
> And stand she erect or bowed,
> Time will win the race he runs with her,
> And hide her away in a shroud.

[363]

A few critics call attention to Rossetti's humorous verses. Anna Bunston de Bary, writing for the *Poetry Review* of May 1912, cites "Frog's Fate" (before 1886) and "Freaks of Fashion" (circa 1878) as two poems in this light-hearted vein.[47]

> *Frog's Fate*
> Contemptuous of his home beyond
> The village and the village-pond,
> A large-souled Frog who spurned
>   each byeway
> Hopped along the imperial highway.
>
> Nor grunting pig nor barking dog
> Could disconcert so great a Frog.
> The morning dew was lingering yet,
> His sides to cool, his tongue to
>   wet:
> The night-dew, when the night
>   should come,

A travelled Frog would send him
    home.

[414]

Freaks of Fashion
Robin says: 'A scarlet waistcoat
    Will be all the wear,
Snug, and also cheerful-looking
    For the frostiest air,
Comfortable for the chest too
    When one comes to plume and
        pair.'

. . . .
Then a Stork took up the word:
    'Aim at height and chic:
Not high heels, they're common;
        somehow
    Stilted legs, not thick,
Not yet thin:' he just glanced
        downward
    And snapped-to his beak.

[396]

Thomas writes, in appreciation of *Sing-Song* (before 1873), that a child likes to view the familiar objects of his experience "in a mood of pleasant wonder, to fancy strange inversions of natural laws or to imagine origins, analogies, far results"; Rossetti gratifies this humorous vein in children by her rhymes without reason and by her poems of beauty and imagination. One such humorous verse that children would laugh at because of "the idiosyncrasies and paradoxical relations of worlds" is "A City Plum Is Not a Plum":

A city plum is not a plum;
A dumb-bell is no bell, though dumb;
A party rat is not a rat'
A sailor's cat is not a cat'
A soldier's frog is not a frog;
A captain's log is not a log.

[427]

(Thomas ventures that these nursery rhymes are an "instance of Christina Rossetti's finding escape from her uneventful well-ordered existence not only into the dream world and into the veiled land beyond death but also into a child's world of wonder, of remarkable and pleasant happenings.")

Although some of Rossetti's animals may be unpleasant to us, Thomas says, "caterpillars and gnats, snails and slugs have to her no more unwelcome suggestions than singing birds and squirrels and butterflies. One is sometimes grateful for little touches of humor which the appearance or the activities of these creatures give,"[48] as in "Twilight Calm" (circa 1850)—

> Screened in the leafy wood
> The stock-doves sit and brood:
> The very squirrel leaps from bough
>   to bough
> But lazily; pauses; and settles now
> Where once he stored his food.
>   . . . .
> The dormouse squats and eats
> Choice little dainty bits
> Beneath the spreading roots of a
>   broad lime;
> Nibbling his fill he stops from time
>   to time
> And listens where he sits.
>
>   [297]

More than half of the critics in this period comment on the meter in Rossetti's poetry. Although most call attention to its unevenness, they find the effect congenial to her work. Ford Madox Hueffer, writing in the March 1904, issue of the *Fortnightly Review*, says that Rossetti's poetry is intricate and rhythmical, although neither musical nor lyrical. But "if it has not the quality of lilt it has not the defect; it is never mechanical with numbered syllables." The quality of the meter in *Sing-Song* is an example:

> Dead in the cold, a song-singing
>   thrush,
> Dead at the foot of a snowberry
>   bush,—
> Weave him a coffin of rush,
> Dig him a grave where the soft
>   mosses grow,
> Raise him a tombstone of snow.
>
>   [427]

Hueffer believes that a child is not concerned with the meaning of verses like these—just as he will sing "London Bridge is broken down" without thinking of the meaning. But children take "a most sensuous pleasure in rhythms of words," and that is the reason why the poems in *Sing-Song* are such favorites with them.[49]

Thomas notes that "a striking and characterizing trait of Christina's stanza form is her habit of closing the stanza with a short line of one or two accents." She admires the effortless lyricism and the fusion of form and subject in Rossetti's work.[50]

Green-Armytage states in *Maids of Honour* that if we read Rossetti's "exquisite" poems carefully, we will often find " 'rhymes' which can only be regarded as *impossible*—poetic freedom in the use of word-sounds which exceeds . . . poetic license." Rossetti's lines he says, are not only "imperfect," but beyond all bounds of "allowable-ness," actually "unscannable." Echoing the judgment of critics of the Victorian era, he says that the irregularity does not matter "when the result is so matchless." The charm of the poetry lies in its sincerity: "The words came straight from her heart to her fingertips. She set the 'essence of poetry' above the form."[51]

Arthur Clutton-Brock, author of *More Essays on Religion* (1927), praises Rossetti's disdain of a preordained pattern of rhythm: "There is a metre, but she is not concerned to keep time with it. . . . The metrical scheme itself is irregular so that it may never become insistent and all obvious cadences are avoided."[52]

George Saintsbury, author of *History of English Prosody* (1910), describes the meter in "Goblin Market" as "a dedoggerelised Skeltonic, utilised in the place of the wooden rattling of the followers of Chaucer. . . . The more the metre is studied the more audacious may its composition seem."[53] He refers especially to the following lines from the poems:

> Morning and evening
> Maids heard the goblins cry:
> 'Come buy our orchard fruits,
> Come buy, come buy:
> Applies and quinces,
> Lemons and oranges,
> Plump unpecked cherries,
> Melons and raspberries,
>
> . . . .
> She clipped a precious golden lock,
> She dropped a tear more rare than pearl,
> Then sucked their fruit globes fair or red.

Sweeter than honey from the rock
Stronger than man-rejoicing wine,
Clearer than water flowed that juice.

[1–2]

Louis Cazamian's *A History of English Literature* also examines the meter of "Goblin Market." Rossetti, he says,

delights in verbal profusion, and the skilful use of metre. . . . Her delicate and shifting impressions are conveyed in a language of easy flow, and develop with the semblance of absolute spontaneity. The vigorous note, the accentuated tone are rare, or scarcely perceptible; and yet the rhythm and the melody of the words are powerfully expressive.[54]

Geoffrey Rossetti believes that "Goblin Market" illustrates Rossetti's mastery of metrical and rhythmical subleties. "The apparent irregularity of the poem is completely ordered and disciplined," and "the variations of pace in the verse are fully controlled." He asks readers to scan these lines:

Laughed every goblin
When they spied her peeping:
Came towards her hobbling,
Flying, running, leaping,
Puffing and blowing,
Chuckling, clapping, crowing,
Clucking and gobbling,
Mopping and mowing,
Full of airs and graces,
Pulling wry faces,
Demure grimaces,
cat-like and rat-like.

[5]

The effect of irregular rhymes in their informal scheme, this Rossetti says, is to hold the reader in suspense, so that the fantastic story seems at times real and at times fantasy. What is more,

The reader may, if he likes, deduce several little moral lessons from the poem, but nowhere is it suggested he should do so. If he chooses to see the goblins, the fruit, the sisters, and the rest as symbols for abstractions, he does so at his own risk. And he risks his enjoyment of the poem.[55]

Hueffer's standard of appreciation is both aesthetic and practical: The meter of "Goblin Market" is short, "its rhymes are concealed enough not to hinder you with a jingle of assonances, and accurate enough to keep the stanzas together":

> At last the evil people,
> Worn out by her resistance,
> Flung back her penny, kicked their fruit
> Along whichever road they took,
> Not leaving root or stone or shoot;
> Some writhed into the ground,
> Some dived into the brook
> With ring and ripple,
> Some scudded on the gale without a sound
> Some vanished in the distance.
>
> [7]

"The whole poem goes in one breath," Hueffner says, but there is so much detail, it gives "the impression of profusion and of value."[56]

Reviewing the poet's prosodic skill in using a variety of musical rhyme schemes—perfect end rhymes, internal rhymes, and imperfect or "partial" rhymes—Geoffrey Rossetti concludes that Rossetti has poetic strength. "Echo," for example, "was surely written with a tune in the mind":

> Come to me in the silence of the night;
>   Come in the speaking silence of a dream;
> Come with soft rounded cheeks and eyes as bright
>   As sunlight on a stream;
>   Come back in tears,
> O memory, hope, love of finished years.
>
> [314]

The complicated rhyme schemes with echoing internal rhymes are not "jingling" or "clumsy." Also to be praised are the monorhymed and solemn poems like "Marvel of Marvels" (before 1893), where the internal echoes of the rhyme within the poem give it "a sense of spaciousness and desolation," as illustrated by the final couplet:

Cold it is, my beloved, since your
        funeral bell was tolled:
Cold it is, O my King, how cold
        alone on the wold.

[123]

The monorhyme in "Heaven Overarches Earth and Sea" (circa
1893), on the other hand, "gives a sense of permanence and cohe-
sion" to the poem:[57]

Heaven overarches earth and sea,
    Earth-sadness and sea-bitterness.
Heaven overarches you and me:
A little while and we shall be—
Please God—where there is no more sea
    Nor barren wilderness

Heaven overarches you and me,
    And all earth's gardens and her graves.
Look up with me, until we see
The day break and the shadows flee.
What though to-night wrecks you and me
    If so to-morrow saves?

[286]

Elisabeth Luther Cary, author of *The Rossettis: Dante Gabriel
and Christina* (1900), asserts that Rossetti's *Monna Innominata*
sonnets, "fourteen nearly perfect examples of the most purely artistic form of verse," illustrate "her instinct for fitness of form by
choosing the noblest and most balanced intellectual structure to
convey her exalted emotion." Although the rhyme endings of
these sonnets are sometimes irregular, the thought and design are
sustained:

While nearly all of the *Monna Innominata* sonnets show two contrasting sides of the intellectual conception, and the sestet forms a kind of
antiphonal response to the octave, the idea is always the outcome of a
fixed emotion, a mighty love in the shadow of renunciation in which
the lighter play of the mind has no part.[58]

This continuity of form gives unity and dignity to the two aspects
of the thought, Cary says, and she summons in evidence the ninth
sonnet:

Thinking of you, and all that was,
    and all
  That might have been and now
    can never be,
  I feel your honoured excellence,
    and see
Myself unworthy of the happier call:
For woe is me who walk so apt to fall,
  So apt to shrink afraid, so apt to
    flee,
  Apt to lie down and die (ah woe
    is me!)
Faithless and hopeless turning to the
    wall
And yet not hopeless quite nor faith-
    less quite,
Because not loveless; love may toil
    all night,
But take at morning; wrestle till
    the break
  Of Day, but then wield power with
    God and man:—
  So take I heart of grace as best I
    can,
Ready to spend and be spent for
    your sake.

                               [61–62]

In the nineteenth century, critics compared Rossetti with the religious poets of the seventeenth century, particularly George Herbert, Robert Herrick, and Henry Vaughan, and such literary figures of their own century as John Henry Newman and John Keble. Comparisons with female poets of her age were few. Some two-thirds of the critics now seek to compare Rossetti's verses with those of her female contemporaries. Although there are differences of opinion as to who was the best versifier, most of the reviewers contend Rossetti vied with—and some say even surpassed—the others.

Muriel Kent, a critic for the slightly left-of-center *Contemporary Review* (incorporating the *Fortnightly*) compares in the December 1930, issue, the poems of Rossetti and Alice Meynell (1847–1922):

While Alice Meynell is pre-eminently a poet for other poets, and is reverenced by scholars, Catholic theologians, and mystics, her concentrated thought—and perhaps her miraculous technique—tends to make her inaccessible to many who find in the poems of Christina Rossetti both "an awakening to lost simplicities" and the cry of their own heart. Equally they are poets of the inner life, and the work of each has the property of illumination; one with the pale radiance of altar candles burning high and clear in a dim cathedral, and the other with a warmer glow, as of a lantern carried through wind and darkness by a human hand.[59]

Alice Meynell herself, as witness her own critique of Rossetti in the previous chapter, would likely agree with Muriel Kent.

There are some comparisons in this period between Rossetti and Emily Dickinson, an American contemporary. For instance, Morton Dauwen Zabel, a reviewer for the New York publication *Poetry* asserts in January 1931: "Between these two women no comparison need be forced. They lived in different worlds, but each found in isolation the fulfillment of high lyrical impulse. . . . Each knew the inexorable laws of personal integrity, and by obeying them, gained her spiritual freedom and her immortality."[60]

But Kathleen C. Green, writing for the December 1930, issue of the *Cornhill Magazine,* a liberal monthly of literature and contemporary concerns, originally edited by the novelist William Makepeace Thackeray, says that Rossetti's work "reads limply, almost flabbily, against the tautness, the dry vigour of Emily Dickinson's thought and execution." In fact, she adds, Mary Coleridge (1861–1906) sounds like Rossetti in some poems, but Miss Coleridge's horror poems are more frightening than Rossetti's.

Green goes on to compare Rossetti's verses with those of Alice Meynell, finding Rossetti's marred by looseness of thought and too frequent sentimentality. Nor do her poems have the "skilful weaving of sounds" we find in those of Victoria Sackville-West, a twentieth-century poet. But in spite of these deficiencies, Green is willing to place Rossetti "in the highest rank of English secondary poets." The secret of "the living power of her poetry," Green says, is that "the purest essence of poetry can only be distilled from a white heat of emotion, and Christina's creative fires, though they burnt inwardly, burnt with consuming force."[61]

Virginia Moore in her *Yale Review* essay of December 1930, compares Rossetti's poetry to that of Emily Dickinson, Charlotte Mew, Elinor Wylie, and Léonie Adams, seeking not a judgment on them but their common bond. It is, she says, their constant renunciation and withdrawal from life's pleasures at great cost. Few men, claims Moore, distrust their natural desires as much as Christina Rossetti, who feared marriage with both James Collinson and Charles Bagot Cayley. "Only a woman, she says," could have written the poetry of Christina Rossetti, with its furious emotional preoccupation—its contradictions, its meekness, its pleasure in pain, its resolution to snare an invisible substance."[62]

During her own lifetime and for several decades after her death, Elizabeth Barrett Browning was considered the best of the Victorian women poets, but the majority of critics who make the comparison in the first half of the new century rate Rossetti's verses higher.

William Henry Hudson, a critic and essayist, writes in his *A Short History of English Literature in the Nineteenth Century* (1918) that Christina Rossetti has the advantage over Elizabeth Barrett Browning in "pure imagination" and in "intensity of poetic vision."[63] Amelia Marjorie Bald, author of *Women-Writers of the Nineteenth Century* (1923), says that "Christina's soul was like a radiant texture, its colours flashing and quivering as if some hidden life were rippling through its folds. Mrs. Browning's soul was of the same colour, but in a paler shade, and woven of plainer threads."[64]

Alexander Hamilton Thomson, in his article about Rossetti in *Cambridge History of English Literature* (1916), asserts that Rossetti was superior to Mrs. Browning in melodiousness of verse.[65] Lafcadio Hearn's *Complete Lectures: A History of English Literature* (1923) calls Rossetti the best woman poet, surpassing Mrs. Browning.[66] John Cunliffe, author of *Leaders of the Victorian Revolution* (1934), also ranks Rossetti as the greatest woman poet of the nineteenth century.[67]

Sir Edward Boyle, a leading critic and author of *Biographical Essays, 1870–1890* (1936), states that although Rossetti's poetry, as that of other fine poets, is more praised than read, the reputations of many of her contemporaries have dwindled in the twentieth century while hers has remained constant. True, she covered a "narrow field," her point of view was always the same, and her poetic powers did not increase toward the end of her life. But, says Boyle, "within the limits which she deliberately set herself few poets, certainly no woman poet, has written in our tongue with the musical and metrical power or with the depth and sensitiveness of feeling which were hers. Within these limits her supremacy remains to-day unchallenged."[68]

Says Frank Jewett Mather, Jr., in the New York *Bookman* of

April 1919: "If the narrowness of Christina Rossetti's outlook makes her a minor poet, surely among the minor singers she is one of the greatest."[69]

Of the reviewers who compare Christina Rossetti with Elizabeth Barrett Browning, almost all point to Rossetti's feminity (read "passivity") as her most estimable characteristic, and the one most lacking in the other's works. Arthur Waugh, author of *Reticence in Literature* (1915) and a prominent critic, makes such a case:

> [Rossetti] was a woman first of all, and she was content to remain a woman to the end. Her poetry, therefore, has no quality more distinguishing than its sincerity. . . ; it accepts the burden of womanhood, and with it the faith, the even, inspiring devotion which is always a true woman's surest weapon. Here, at once, she separates from her great contemporary among women, poets, Elizabeth Barrett Browning. For, when we come to inquire why it is that so much of Mrs. Browning's poetry, with its fiery eloquence, and its "headlong" advocacy of cause and reform, proves upon nearer acquaintance so unsatisfying, we are more and more assured that she fails because she is trying . . . to make a woman's voice thunder like a man's. Christina Rossetti made no such mistake in art, permitted herself no such liberties with artistic sincerity. Her devotional poetry is the poetry of a devout woman; not of a Paul, nor of an Apollos. She does not preach; she lays down no lines for others to follow; she simply folds her hands before the altar lights, and lifts her eyes to the rood. And criticism itself grows silent before the prospect of a woman praying.[70]

Almost twenty years later Edward Thomas, author of *The Last Sheaf* (1938), makes the same judgment, if less eloquently: "By reason of her very weakness; . . . by her femininity," Christina Rossetti recommends herself. Mrs. Browning was more energetic: "she wrote poems which demand comparison with those of men; and she failed." Since Rossetti competed with no man, "she is the greatest of the women among our poets."[71]

Paul Elmer More, a leading critic for the Boston-based the *Atlantic Monthly*, which offered its readers exposés of corruption in government and political and social commentary as well as literary criticism, claims in the December 1904, issue that Rossetti, despite the narrowness of her range of subjects, deserves greater praise than Browning, and he offers many of the same reasons cited by Waugh and Thomas. In the case of Mrs. Browning, he asserts, there was "an unreconciled feud between her intellect and her heart. She had neither a woman's wise passivity nor a man's controlling will."

Critic More adds that most women will consider Mrs. Browning a paragon of her sex, while most men will believe that the honor belongs to Rossetti:

> Women will judge a poetess by her inclusion of the larger human nature, and will resent the limiting of her range to the qualities that we look upon as peculiarly feminine. The passion of Mrs. Browning, her attempt to control her inspiration to the demands of a shaping intellect, her questioning and answering, her larger aims, in a word her effort to create—all these will be set down to her credit by women who are as appreciative of such qualities as men, and who will not be annoyed by the false tone running through them. Men, on the contrary, are apt, in accepting a woman's work or in creating a female character, to be interested more in the traits and limitations which distinguish her from her masculine complement. They care more for the idea of a woman, and less for woman as merely a human being . . . though I am aware of the ridicule to which such an opinion lays me open; and for the same reason I hold that Christina Rossetti is a more complete exemplar of feminine genius, and, as being more perfect in her own sphere, a better poet than Mrs. Browning.[72]

It is this "passive attitude towards the powers that command her heart and her soul," More says, that makes Rossetti "the purest expression in English of the feminine genius," and it is this passivity that differentiates her from masculine mystic poets:

> Read the masculine poets who have heard this mystic call of the spirit, and you feel yourself in the presence of a strong will that has grasped the world, and, finding it insufficient, deliberately casts it away; and there is no room for pathetic regret in their ruthless determination to renounce. But this womanly poet does not properly renounce at all, she passively allows the world to glide away from her. The strength of her genius is endurance.[73]

George Lowther, a critic for the *Contemporary Review* of November 1913, asserts, too, that Rossetti has a true religious sense which he finds lacking among men:

> Men are so apt to confound frivolity with merriment, and melancholy with religion; so strange do they find the paradoxes of the Faith that they are fain to turn away from all that reminds them of a Strait Path. . . . Men love what they are pleased to fancy their freedom, and

think that a settled spiritual purpose must needs be an irksome companion.[74]

The judgment is not that of men alone. Elizabeth Luther Cary, author of *The Rossettis* (1900), relates that Dante Gabriel Rossetti, writing to Christina about her poetry, warned her to avoid "a falsetto muscularity of style." But Cary claims that her brother's anxiety was unwarranted. "The quality of Christina's imagination and the quality of her expression are alike feminine. Even her thoughts are restricted to the single round of 'woman's sphere,' . . . loving and grieving and praying." As further evidence of the poet's feminity, "we find in her poetry neither politics nor socialism nor pedantry."[75]

A. J. Green-Armytage has a bone to pick with such views. In his *Maids of Honour* (1906) he directly takes on Watts Dunton, who had written in the *Athenaeum* ten years earlier that the Christian idea is "essentially feminine."

> Is self-sacrifice and devotion to an ideal "essentially feminine"? Are the men "of whom the world was not worthy" only abnormal specimens? . . . Does Mr. Watts Dunton leave it to be inferred that all the highest attributes of human nature—faith, mercy, purity, truth—belong exclusively to feminity? If it be so, then surely the meekest of her sex may take courage, for it must follow, as the night the day, that at some time or other woman will come into her kingdom. . . . The only thing to wait for is the day when a sufficient number of the male creation can be brought to agree with his dogmatic and enigmatic assertion.

True, Green-Armytage continues, woman has always been "more keenly alive than man to the beauty of holiness," either in the "abstract or the concrete." But to admit the thesis that "Christianity is 'essentially feminine' . . . would be to admit that it is unmanly; and the Christ of the Bible is a very manly Christ, as well as a Godlike man."[76]

Green-Armytage is not alone in fighting the previous century's battles. Unlike Green-Armytage, though, and in the minority among the critics of the period, are those who go the barricades to demand equality in the literary marketplace. One such defender of equal opportunity is Ford Madox Hueffer, prominent author, essayist, and intimate of the Rossettis, whose essay in the *Fortnightly Review* (1904) received earlier mention. In *Memories and Impressions,* a work published in 1911, he gives vent to remembered anger

Dante Gabriel Rossetti, a self-portrait, 1855.

at John Ruskin, a leading critic of Rossetti's day, who had tried to convince the poet not to write because she would be competing with her painter-poet brother, Dante Gabriel, and might do damage to his fame or market. At confronting such an attitude, Hueffer says, "I am filled with as hot and as uncontrollable an anger as I am when faced by some more than usually imbecile argument against the cause of women's franchise."[77]

To an anonymous reviewer for the *Times Literary Supplement* on November 14, 1929, "the clearest eye and hand in all the [Pre-Raphaelite] circle belonged to Christina Rossetti, but because she was a woman, her influence was merely negative. The defeat of Christina Rossetti was a judgment on the success of her associates."[78]

Other critics—and, indeed, almost a third of those who address Christina Rossetti's work in this period compare her efforts with those of Dante Gabriel—find much that differs in the work and outlook of the two siblings. A typical contrast between the two is provided by Mr. and Mrs. Hugh Walker in their *Outlines of Victorian Literature* (1919):

> He is sensuous and gorgeous while her verse is refined and simple. She stands straining her eyes towards heaven, while he makes the Blessed Damozel gaze back with yearning from heaven to earth. To him the Oxford Movement meant a revival of colour and beauty, to her it meant greater opportunity for suffering. Her attitude was that of Newman. Her brother found in the middle ages merely material for the art that was his religion.[79]

A. J. Green-Armytage notes that Christina Rossetti was revolted by Mariolatry but that Dante Gabriel, "whose love of symbolism exceeded her own, but who . . . had no leanings whatever towards the adoption of the Roman Church—considered that the weak point of Anglicanism was its rejection of the womanly element from its creed, which this doctrine necessarily involves."[80]

There are numerous attempts in this period, too, to relate Christina Rossetti's poetry to the Romantic tradition. Fredegond Shove, author of *Christina Rossetti: A Study* (1931), for example, compares the poet's nursery rhymes in *Sing-Song* to Blake's *Songs of Innocence:* Rossetti, in the Blake tradition, shows "her love and veneration for innocence—children, lambs, birds, dogs, cats, rabbits, caterpillars, flowers and sea beasts":[81]

On the grassy banks
Lambkins at their pranks;
Woolly sisters, woolly brothers,
    Jumping off their feet,
While their woolly mothers
    Watch by them and bleat.

[429]

And here:

Rushes in a watery place,
    And reeds in a hollow;
A soaring skylark in the sky,
    A daring swallow
And where pale blossom used to hang
    Ripe fruit to follow.

[429]

Eleanor Thomas states in her 1931 biography of Rossetti that "fishes with umbrellas and her lizards with parasols recall Alice's adventures through the looking glass":[82]

When fishes set umbrellas up
    If the rain-drops run,
Lizards will want their parasols
    To shade them from the sun.

[434]

What is more, says Thomas, when Rossetti wrote her ghost poems, she "was following one of the strong romantic currents of the nineteenth century,"[83] for Victorian poets, like the Romantics, wrote supernatural or folk superstition verses because they wished to escape from their prosaic world to a more remote or exotic one and enjoyed imagining that they were beings from another world.

Thomas is even able to find "many echoes in [Rossetti's] poetry of the language of the King James Bible, her own attendant phrases being scarcely distinguishable in style from the Biblical quotation." The simplicity of Rossetti's style, she says, "becomes in a few instances the quaintness of seventeenth-century religious verse."[84]

Shove finds Rossetti "like George Herbert in her conversations with her Lord, and like the holy anchoress of Norwich, the Lady Juliana, in her deep sense of the marvel of the redemption."[85]

Oliver Elton, author of *A Survey of English Literature* (1926), remarks that "the curious tracking down of a thought, or scruple, or image, even to the point of quaintness, recalls the tradition of Anglican poetry in George Herbert or Henry Vaughan." But all in all Rossetti is a unique poet, "unswayed by any of the religious poets of her own century, Keble or Heber, or any or whom, or perhaps all together, she excels in endowment."[86]

Expect no such discourses on Rossetti's verses from me, Edwardian literary courtier Sir Walter Raleigh confides in a letter published among his collected letters in 1926:

> I think she is the best poet alive. . . . The worse of it is you cannot lecture on really pure poetry any more than you can talk about the ingredients of pure water—it is adulterated, methylated, sanded poetry that makes the best lectures. The only thing that Christina make me want to do, is cry, not lecture.[87]

With publication of William Michael's "Memoir" to *The Poetical Works* in 1906 we note the heightened interest of critics in Rossetti's secular poems, predominately the posthumously published *New Poems*. These critics, among them a growing number of women, express their empathy with the poet's sufferings, but some go further, questioning the traditions and self-imposed constraints that appear to have fueled Rossetti's torment. Memorable here is Sister Madeleva's praise for the poet's "patient sweetness," hand in hand with the judgment that "her homesickness for heaven is near to hypochondria."[88]

At the century's beginning we see Rossetti's "worldly" poems vying for attention with the devotional poems that were so popular in the previous one. Somewhat later—arguably the result of the publication, by a number of women, of biographies of the poet—interest in the secular works became greater by far. One also remarks the drastic falling off of reviews in the religious press in the same period. Perhaps here too William Michael's "Memoir" had done its work, revealing to those who would cherish a poet-saint, a poet-woman who was at least as much Eve as Mary.

The relative wealth of biographical matter after the poverty of detail in the previous century and the development of a psychoanalytic approach to criticism emboldened reviewers to search for deeper meanings in some poems than had been ventured before. Oliver Elton's reading of "Goblin Market"—"a good fairy tale, with a latent note of mischief, sadism, and paint"—and Eleanor Thomas's of the same verses—"the extreme lusciousness of the fruit suggests the allurement of sin"—which owe much to these new currents, adds to appreciation of Rossetti's works.

In common with their counterparts of the Victorian era, critics of this period are wont to examine the poet's unorthodox rhythmic patterns and, in much the same terms, to applaud their overall effect.

The year 1930, the centennial of Christina Rossetti's birth, brought an upsurge of literary criticism that often surveyed the poet's place in the literary firmament. Though this lacked the testimonial quality of the Victorian century, most critics were in agreement that the works offered rich rewards for the twentieth-century reader, even "whilst" some, as Shove recognized, were "remaining chill to her passionate Christianity."

The numerous articles in which Christina Rossetti was compared with female contemporaries, a hallmark of this period, served to flatter the poet and add to her reputation. However, the genre itself suffers from a tendency to critical bias and a disregard of much of the complexity of sound and sense in the poetical works—as much in the case of Rossetti as in that of the poets with whom she was compared favorably.

A womanly poet or a poet who happened to be a woman? Fires lighted in the last century burned at the beginning of this one, emitting more heat than light. Paul Elmer More, for instance, though aware "of the ridicule to which such an opinion lays [him] open," contended that men "care more for the idea of a woman, and less for woman as merely a human being." But from all evidence, the ultimate judgment of Christina Rossetti's work will not hinge upon whether hers or Elizabeth Browning's is the better voice for its femininity or seeming abjurance of femininity. Rather, that judgment will be rendered on her quality as an artist.

3

The Poet Psychoanalyzed: Criticism, 1940–1982

The new psychological systems made possible much more methodical approaches. One could analyze a particular work and draw from the analysis inferences about the psychology of its author; one could take the whole body of an author's writing and derive from it general conclusions about his state of mind which could then be applied to elucidate particular works. One could take the biography of a writer, as illustrated by the external events of his life and . . . construct out of these a theory of the writer's personality—his conflicts, frustrations, traumatic experiences, neuroses, or whatever they happened to be—and use this theory in order to illuminate each one of his works. Or can one work back and forth between the life and the work, illuminating each by the other, noting from the biography certain crises reflected in the works, and seeing from the way they are reflected in the works what their real biographical meaning was.

David Daiches, *Critical Approaches to Literature*

Freud and Jung have shown that pools and fountains are symbolic of fulfillment used by individuals whose lives are inhibited or dried up. How natural, then for Christina Rossetti, whose inhibitions and self-denials had already become a mark of her character, to express joy in images of sensual gratification.

Conrad Festa, *English Language Notes*

A special female self-awareness emerges through literature in every period.

Patricia Ann Meyer Spacks, *The Female Imagination*

107

*T*he approximately one hundred and forty critical reviews of
Christina Rossetti's works that have appeared since 1940 take the
form of essays, introductions to editions of selected works, biographies and criticism of these biographies, and dissertations. These
reviews are preponderantly a mix of biography and criticism—
exemplifying the "methodological approach" that is characterized
above by David Daiches.

The poems that came under most frequent scrutiny during this
period were the long narrative poems—"Goblin Market," "The
Prince's Progress," "A Royal Princess," "Maiden Song," and
"From House to Home"—which offer visions of remote and en-
chanted worlds; the *Monna Innominata* sonnet sequence, along
with "A Birthday," and "A Triad," which range over love's emotional spectrum from ecstasy to grief; the lyrical poems—
"Remember," "When I Am Dead, My Dearest," "Oh Roses for
the Flush of Youth," "An End," "A Pause," and "Sleeping at
Last"—with their twin themes of love and death; the dream
poems—"My Dream," "A Nightmare," "Dream-Love," "Echo,"
and "Dream Land"; the whimsical animal characterization poems—
"A Venus Seems My Mouse," "The Blindest Buzzard That I
Know," and "A Pig Wore a Wig" (a nursery rhyme from *Sing-
Song;* and the ghost poems—"The Poor Ghost," "At Home," "The
Hour and the Ghost"; and the dramatic poems—"Twice," "Eve,"
"Sister Maude," "Noble Sisters," and "Convent Threshold." On
the infrequent occasions when Rossetti's poems of spiritual con-
tent receive more than passing notice, it is the perennial favorites—
"Amor Mundi," "Up-hill," "A Better Resurrection," "The Heart
Knoweth Its Own Bitterness," "Long Barren," "Old and New
Year Ditties," and "The Lowest Place"—that have recommended
themselves to recent critics.

Among the few contemporary critics who closely examine Rossetti's devotional poems and other verses of spiritual content is
Margaret Sawtell, author of *Christina Rossetti: Her Life and Religion* (1955). Sawtell considers Rossetti to have put the spiritual
love of God higher than the love of man, for surely the poet makes
this clear in Sonnet 6 of the *Monna Innominata* series. Here, notes
Sawtell, Rossetti says in "clear language . . . that God and His Will
matter more than the most passionate most possessive love that
man may conceive, with the corollary, that provided that divine
love has priority, one cannot love a friend too much":[1]

> Trust me, I have not earned your dear rebuke,
> I love, as you would have me, God the most. . . .

> Yet while I love my God the most, I deem
> That I can never love you overmuch.
>   I love Him more, so let me love you too.
> Yea, as I apprehend it, love is such
> I cannot love you if I love not Him.
>   I cannot love Him if I love not you.[2]

Sawtell claims that Rossetti renounced her earthly lovers because "she had arrived at a perfectly clear conclusion—that married love was not for her, that God was still claiming her sole allegiance . . . once her will was set to that purpose, other loves might have a place, but a very secondary one." When Rossetti had come to that conclusion, there were still a few cries of weakness, despondency, and self-reproach. But her later devotional poems illustrate "an ever-growing and never questioned trust in the faithfulness of Jesus, no matter how great the weakness or faithlessness of the beloved."[3] Witness "Wrestling" (before 1875):

> Alas my Lord
> How should I wrestle all the live-
>   long night
> With Thee my God, my strength
>   and my delight?
>
>   . . . .
>
>   Lord, give me strength
> To hold Thee fast until we see Thy
>   Face
> Full fountain of all rapture and all
>   grace.
>
> [247]

What Sawtell dubs a liberating faith, a few others have called piteous and sure to reap unhappiness. "Up-hill" (1858)—praised by critics of earlier periods for the sincerity of its faith that, although the virtuous path is long and arduous, the traveler will find everlasting joy and comfort in God's inn at the summit—is called by one modern reviewer a horror poem. It is "more sinister than the melodramatic flesh-creepings of Edgar Allen Poe," writes F. L. Lucas in her essay "Christina Rossetti" in *Ten Victorian Poets* (1940). An Anglo-Saxon grave-poem—" 'for thee was a house built, ere that thou born wert' "—comes to her mind, and she visualizes the end of "Up-hill" to be, not the heaven Rossetti yearned for, but the house of death, the grave. "It was in her own flesh that she hammered home and nails," Lucas concludes. "For lack of a little more feather-pated gaiety, her life became a thing grim to contemplate." Rossetti's conscience and her superego acted as scourging dictators: "The fate of Christina Rossetti is a thing to shudder at."[4]

Whether her life was "grim," "virtuous," or filled with "self-reproach," what were its significant events and dominating emotions, and how are these reflected in Christina Rossetti's poetry? Interest in the poet's biography as a means of illuminating her work has grown and shows no signs of abatement in these forty years. Methods of applying such insights range from what David Daiches calls in *Critical Approaches to Literature* "the older 'bio-critical approach' "—in which "the psychology of the author concerned is related . . . to the special features of his work"[5]—to what Susan Sontag has characterized most unsympathetically in *Against Interpretation* (1966) as a process of "excavation"—"it digs 'behind' the text, to find a subtext which is the true one."[6]

Stuart Curran provides an example of the "older" approach in his contribution to the Autumn 1971 American publication *Victorian Poetry*.[7] The striking events of Rossetti's life, he asserts, gave impetus to "The Convent Threshold" (1858), a poem in which the speaker has given up her earthly lover and enters a convent to expiate sins of the flesh:

> For all night long I dreamed of you:
> I woke and prayed against my will,
> Then slept to dream of you again.
> At length I rose and knelt and prayed.
> I cannot write the words I said,
> My words were slow, my tears were few;
> But through the dark my silence spoke
> Like thunder. When this morning broke,
> My face was pinched, my hair was grey,
> And frozen blood was on the sill
> Where stifling in my struggle I lay.

> [342]

For F. L. Lucas, "From House to Home" (1858)—a poem in which the speaker, rejecting all earthly pleasures, suffers intensely from such renunciation but is promised by a mysterious voice " 'You shall meet again, / Meet in a distant land' "—recalls the ordeal Rossetti underwent when, soon after breaking off her engagement to Collinson, she met him near Regent's Park and fainted from the shock:[8]

That night destroyed me like an
    avalanche;
  One night turned all my summer
    back to snow:
Next morning not a bird upon my
    branch,
  Not a lamb woke below,—

. . . .

Azure and sun were starved from
    heaven above,
  No dew had fallen, but biting
    frost lay hoar:
O love, I knew that I should meet
  Should I find my love no more.

. . . .

These thorns are sharp, yet I can
    tread on them;
  This cup is loathsome, yet He
    makes it sweet:
My face is steadfast toward
    Jerusalem,
  My heart remembers it.

[22–25]

C. M. Bowra contends in *The Romantic Imagination* (1961) that "In perfect innocence [Rossetti] would write poems which are to all appearances dramatic lyrics about imaginary situations, but which nonetheless show unmistakable traces of her own feelings and sufferings."[9]

Marya Zaturenska asserts in her *Christina Rossetti: A Portrait with Background* (1949) that the *Monna Innominata* sonnet sequence (before 1882), was a monument to Rossetti's love for Charles Bagot Cayley and that her renunciation of him is expressed in the sixth sonnet, which mingles mysticism, pathos, austerity, love, and stubborn denial. This is the sonnet which Sawtell saw as expressing the poet's spiritual love of God. For Zaturenska, it is one in which "we can almost hear her voice—she is talking to Cayley and not through a book but with the living voice."[10]

Georgina Battiscombe, in *Christina Rossetti: A Divided Life* (1981), indicates that Rossetti's own family is reflected in "The Prince's Progress" (1861–65). The Prince—"his careless physical prowess as opposed to his moral weakness—'strong of limb if of purpose weak'—is Dante Gabriel [Rossetti's brother] . . . while . . . the waiting Princess pining slowly away as her lover dallies and delays suggests Lizzie [Elizabeth Siddal, Rossetti's sister-in-law] and her increasing ill health during the years of waiting before her marriage" to him.[11]

Battiscombe also theorizes that "Cousin Kate" (1859) reflects the experience Rossetti obtained while working from 1860 to 1870 at the House of Charity at Highgate, a penitentiary for "fallen women" run by Anglican nuns, and the poet's "concern for the unmarried mother."[12] In the poem, a " 'a cottage maiden' " has been seduced and abandoned by " 'a great lord' ":

> He lured me to his palace-home—
> Woe's me for joy thereof—
> To lead a shameless shameful life
> His plaything and his love.

Her cousin Kate, however, resisted the lord's advances and held out for marriage:

> Because you were so good and pure
> He bound you with his ring:
> The neighbours call you good and
>   pure,
> Call me an outcast thing.

But the fallen woman has a gift denied the barren wife:

> My fair-haired son, my shame, my
>   pride,
> Cling closer, closer yet;
> Your sire would give broad lands for one
> To wear his coronet.

>   [347]

Many modern critics find elements of biography even in two of Rossetti's animal characterizations, "A Sketch" (1864) and "A Venus Seems My Mouse" (1877), a number believing both of them refer to Cayley, the suitor of her mature years. Zaturenska relates that Cayley had picked up a sea mouse while vacationing at the shore and sent it in a bottle to the poet as a special bid for her favor, knowing that she would appreciate such a curiosity as much as he did. Ostensibly Rossetti wrote "A Venus Seems My Mouse" as a "thank you" note. Zaturenska characterizes the poem as "full of tenderness and unaccustomed humor. . . . Does she not somehow identify Cayley himself with the sea mouse?"[13]

A Venus seems my Mouse
Come safe ashore from foaming seas . . .

A darling Mouse it is:
Part hope not likely to take wing . . .

From shifting tides set safe apart,
In no mere bottle, in my heart
Keep house.

[444]

Georgina Battiscome, in an earlier work, *Christina Rossetti* (1965), also associates "A Sketch" with Cayley. This was the man with whom the poet fell in love, Battiscome states, and he with her, "although he seems to have been a singularly ineffectual lover." This poem is "an affectionate but slightly exasperated"[14] verse in which the poet likens her suitor to a buzzard and a mole:

My blindest buzzard that I know,
    My special mole, when will you see?
    Oh no, you must not look at me
There's nothing hid for me to show.
I might show facts as plain as day:
But, since your eyes are blind, you'd say,
    'Where? What?' and turn away.

[369]

But the buzzard's nest gets a bit crowded. Lona Mosk Packer, author of *Christina Rossetti* (1963), offers the thesis that the pious Christina Rossetti loved a married man, William Bell Scott, an artist-poet friend of her brother Dante Gabriel. Packer assumes that Rossetti did not know Scott was married when she met him and fell in love; at being apprised of Scott's marital status, Rossetti refused to continue the love affair. But, says Packer, the heartbreak of this event, commingled with a continuing and guilty love, was the source of the great suffering and despair evident in so many of Rossetti's works.[15]

For Packer too, "A Sketch" is "transparently autobiographical," but her candidate for the "blindest buzzard" is Scott, who continued to misread the poet's message of love—not because he was "incapable of seeing but because it was his conscious policy to shut his eyes to her meaning."[16]

However, William E. Fredeman, writing in the September 1964, issue of *Victorian Studies,* a quarterly journal of the humanities, arts, and sciences, discounts Packer's hypothesis that Rossetti's poetry reflects a deep personal conflict because of her frustrated love for Scott. "Circumstantial evidence derived primarily from the poetry makes impossible the precise documentation of a theory for which there is not a single scrap of positive and direct proof," he declares. Although Packer's "insights into the poetry are original and illuminating" and her biography makes "an important contribution to Rossetti's studies, . . . at best the case for Scott is not strong."[17]

Nesca A. Robb, author of *Four in Exile* (1948), considers it "an unprofitable question" even to guess at the relation of Rossetti's verses and her life experiences.

> The lost lover . . . is nowhere individualised. Impersonal as air, more bodiless than any ghost, he is like a character in a play who is continually talked about and who influences the action, but who never himself appears on the stage. We see the reactions he provokes in the writer, never the person who provokes them. Her pain, her disillusionment, her memories, are poignantly vivid, but any attempt at portraying the beloved remains ineffectual.[18]

Jerome J. McGann considers the very elusiveness of personal data to add strength to Rossetti's work and to have been cultivated by the poet herself. Writing in the Winter 1980, issue of *Victorian Studies,* he maintains that Rossetti uses the personal secret as a symbol of individuality: "Independence is a function of the ability to have a secret which the sanctioned forces of society can not invade." The speakers in "Winter: My Secret" (1857)—

> I tell my secret? No indeed, not I:
> Perhaps some day, who knows?
> But not today'
>
> [336]

—and "No, Thank You, John" (1860)

> Here's friendship for you if you
> like, but love—
> No, thank you, John.
>
> [349]

—politely refuse to sacrifice their individuality. "In that reserve of purpose lies Christina Rossetti's power, her secret, her very self."[19]

Most reviewers in the contemporary period see an apparent tug-of-war between "the woman and the saint"—as C. M. Bowra characterizes the contenders in the life and works of the poet—and seek its roots. "The conflict in Christina," says Bowra,

> was hers almost till the end, though with the passing of years her religion became more absorbing and more insistent and allowed her only at intervals to indulge her more human feelings. . . . In her religious hours she believed that the world was a nothing, and she would regret her lost chances and her vanishing dreams. She would indeed accept her fate, but not altogether willingly and not without regret.[20]

Packer and others see the conflict in even starker terms: the poems earlier praised for their exemplary piety draw on elements of both religiosity and unconscious erotic longing. In "The Heart Knoweth Its Own Bitterness" (1857), according to Packer, these two strains reflect the torment of the period immediately following Rossetti's termination of her relationship with Scott. He, it happens, was distracted by the many attractive women about him and had obviously forgotten the poet; in the poem, "using the symbolic languge of religious eroticism, the speaker castigates with all-too-human resentment the earthly lover who has failed her":[21]

> I long for one to stir my deep—
>   I have had enough to help and gift—
>   I long for one to search and sift
> Myself, to take myself and keep.
>
> You scratch my surface with your pin,
>   You stroke me smooth with hushing breath:
> Nay pierce, nay probe, and dig within,
>   Probe my quick core and sound my depth.
> You call me with a puny call,
>   You talk, you smile, you nothing do:
>   How should I spend my heart on you,
> My heart that so outweighs you all?
>
> [192]

Another poem that some reviewers relate to the presumed important events in Rossetti's life is "Twice" (1874). Packer, for example, in calling this poem inspired by fact, not fancy, indicates that the lover who rejects the speaker is Scott. In fact, the poem's title, "Twice," alludes "as plainly as poetic language can to two loves, one human and the other divine."[22] When the earthly lover spurns the narrator, then and only then does she offer her hand to God:

> I take my heart in my hand—
>   I shall not die, but live—
> Before Thy face I stand;
>   I, for Thou callest such:
> All that I have I bring,
>   All that I am I give;
> Smile Thou and I shall sing,
>   But shall not question much.
>
> [367]

Some critics believe that Rossetti chose spinsterhood over marriage out of a conviction that, in giving herself to her husband, she would be sullied before God and the door to Paradise would be irrevocably shut against her. For example, for Georgina Battiscombe in her 1965 work, the same lines of "The Heart Knoweth Its Own Bitterness" that Packer cites as having been inspired by Scott make "clear that this shrinking [from marriage with either one of her suitors, Collinson or Cayley] was no commonplace horror of sexual intimacy; it was not the nature but the demands of the flesh which made her turn away to another love."[23] In her 1981 study, Battiscombe points to the same sort of "human anguish" in some of Rossetti's religious poems: "For Christina there was no deep division between *eros* and *agape,* love human and love divine: she saw the two as very closely akin. There is a curious and touching purity in her *eros* feeling; there is passion in her conception of *agape.*"[24] This is reflected in "A Better Resurrection" (1857):

> I have no wit, no words, no tears;
>   My heart within me like a stone
> Is numbed too much for hopes or fears.
>   Look right, look left, I dwell alone: . . .
> I lift mine eyes, but dimmed with grief
>   No everlasting hills I see;
> My life is in the falling leaf;
>   O Jesus, quicken me.
>
> [191]

To C. M. Bowra, too, there was "something very deep in [Rossetti's] nature, something which made her shrink from the claims of the flesh." But "it was more than an unusual fastidiousness, even more than a desire to keep herself unspotted from the world":

> It was a deep conviction that she was dedicated to God and that any concession to the body would be an act of disloyalty to Him. Her religion imposed duties so imperative that she could not compromise with them, but, more than that, it made even marriage an impossibility. Love she knew and exercised with all the strength of her gentle, devoted nature, but deep in her something turned her away from any call which summoned her to give to a human being what must be kept for God.[25]

Geoffrey Grigson, writing in the *Times Literary Supplement* for April 11, 1980, claims that Rossetti is trapped "between flesh and spirit, between two kinds of love, one of them coupled with sin and punishment." Her poems emerge from "the clash of loyalties"; the better poems are those of defeated love, the lesser poems are those of didactic piety.[26]

Germaine Greer concludes in her introduction to a 1975 edition of *Goblin Market* that Rossetti's sexuality embarrassed her and made her agonizingly self-conscious; "Appalled by the uncontrollable violence of her own nature, Rossetti resolved to stifle herself, no matter what the cost, even though she could not conjure up before her soul's eye any clear picture of what her reward for such relentless self-abuse might be."[27]

Some critics discern a longing for love not only in Rossetti's dramatic poems, but in the nursery rhymes of *Sing-Song* (1872) as well. For example, in *Wonder and Whimsy* (1960), Thomas Burnett Swann points to his favorite piece in the volume, "Twist Me a Crown of Wind-Flowers," which expresses to him Rossetti's own yearnings for the refuge of a perfect love. The first speaker cries out:

> 'Twist me a crown of wind-flowers;
>   That I may fly away
> To hear the singers at their song,
>   And players at their play.'

[430]

But Swann notes that the second speaker, the voice of reality, reminds the first that wind-flowers last only a day, as if to say that perfect love is unobtainable:[28]

'Alas! your crown of wind-flowers
Can never make you fly:
I twist them in a crown to-day,
and to-night they die.'

[413]

In analyzing a literary work, David Daiches maintains in *Critical Approaches to Literature,* "the critic is often led into psychology, into a discussion of the state of mind out of which literary creation arises."[29] Several reviewers deal with this aspect of criticism in their investigations of the erotic quality of Rossetti's dream poems. Packer takes on "My Dream" (1855), in which the speaker relates a dream in which a destructive, savage, and carnal crocodile grows fat devouring all the other crocodiles:

An execrable appetite arose,
He battened on them, crunched, and sucked them in,
He knew no law, he feared no binding law,
But ground them with inexorable jaw.
The luscious fat distilled upon his chin,
Exuded from his nostrils and his eyes,
While still like hungry death he fed his maw;
Till, every minor crocodile being dead
And buried too, himself gorged to the full,
He slept with breath oppressed and unstrung claw.

[315]

Rossetti is "substituting one sort of sensuous appetite for another, a common form of displacement in dreams," Packer maintains. She wonders if Rossetti has not used the sensual crocodile to represent William Bell Scott; or perhaps it is the libertine Scott, who, in following his own appetites, exercised no moral restraint whatsoever. The gastro-metabolic image, Packer feels, is Rossetti's mode of describing a love relationship.[30] But Georgina Battiscombe says in her 1981 study that if there is to be a sexual interpretation of "My Dream"—which "may well be the correct one—the crocodile must be taken as representing the Male in general, not any particular man."[31]

Packer finds eroticism in some of the childlike rhymes of *Sing-Song.* She considers "Heartsease in My Garden Bed" yet another reference to Scott:

Heartsease in my garden bed,
With sweetwilliam white and red.

> Honeysuckle on my wall:—
> Heartsease blossoms in my heart
> When sweet William comes to call;
> But it withers when we part,
> And the honey-trumpet fall.
>
> [430]

"Heartsease," Packer points out, was "a flower which appears in Scott's early verse as an erotic symbol," and it is juxtaposed with "sweet William, with its punning allusion to both flower and lover."[32]

Several modern critics seek to uncover in Rossetti's dream poems evidence of the poet's unconscious erotic longings. Here Sigmund Freud's theory of the dream is brought into play. As interpreted by Lionel Trilling in *The Liberal Imagination: Essays on Literature and Society* (1953), Freud saw the dream as the unconscious "effort to reconstruct the bad situation in order that the failure to meet it may be recouped; in these dreams there is no obscured intent to evade but only an attempt to meet the situation, to make a new effort of control."[33]

Ralph A. Bellas, author of *Christina Rossetti* (1977), pursues this theory, asserting that in Rossetti's dream poems "past love often becomes indistinguishable from a dream love. Since past love—and that unfulfilled—is only a memory, it can be given a semblance of reality only as a dream; that is, to be called forth by the imagination." He cites "Song" (1851), "What?" (1853), "Dream-Love" (1854), "Long Looked For" (1854), "Echo" (1854), and "For One Sake" (1857) as poems of past and dreamed love. To Bellas, "the dream or imaginative experience serves as a palliative for frustrated love."[34]

Another dream poem in which some critics find evidence of unconscious erotic longings is "Nightmare" (1857). Rossetti's brother William Michael, in his "Memoir" and "Notes" to the *Poetical Works of Christina Georgina Rossetti* (1906), tells us that in his sister's notebook this three-page composition starts on page 25 and ends on page 27 but that the intermediate leaf had been destroyed. "Mere scrap as it is," he states, "I should be sorry to lose it quite."[35] The poem, as it appears in the *Poetical Works,* concerns a haunting ghost:

> I have a friend in ghostland—
> Early found, ah me how early lost!—
> Blood-red seaweeds drip along that coastland
> By the strong sea wrenched and tost.

> If I wake he haunts me like a nightmare:
> I feel my hair stand up, my body creep:
> Without a light I see a blasting sight there,
> See a secret I must keep.

[333]

Packer calls attention to the fact that there were two revealing words in the poet's manuscript [Rossetti's notebooks for the years 1842–66 are in the Bodleian Library, Oxford] that William Michael saw fit to change in the printed text. The first line originally read, "I have a *love* in ghostland," and the fifth line, "If I wake he *rides* me like a nightmare." Packer suggests that the original words can be seen to reveal the passion seething in Rossetti.[36]

Unconscious longings? Quite the contrary, says Cora Kaplan in "The Indefinite Disclosed: Christina Rossetti and Emily Dickinson" in *Women Writing and Writing About Women* (1979). For Rossetti the dream poems offer an opportunity to express quite conscious longings. "Christina Rossetti used dream-form as a favourite device when she wanted to exempt her poems from the demands of clarity; . . . the dream-state . . . permits the expression of feelings and the enactment of dramas taboo in genteel households. . . . " 'My Dream,' " Kaplan says, "deflects analysis" though "overloaded with symbols—heathen, phallic, and patriarchal—but they are as elusive as a gnomic folk tale."[37]

Rossetti's frequent theme of love terminated by early death interests a number of critics, several of whom, echoing most of the critics of the Victorian era, consider its source to be the poet's general wish for peace and rest. For example, Nesca A. Robb in *Four in Exile* (1948) notes that "sometimes Christina sees death as a timeless peace, a suspension of all strife though not of all consciousness,"[38] as in "Rest" (1849):

> Darkness more clear than noonday holdeth her,
> Silence more musical than any song.

[293]

and "Dream Land" (1849):

> Rest, rest at the heart's core
> Till time shall cease:

[292]

Others, such as Marya Zaturenska in *Christina Rossetti: A Portrait with Background* (1949), wonder whether Rossetti's sadness in the poems that seem suffused with the pain of unconsummated love and the prospect of death might not stem from physical as well as emotional causes. "How much of this was due to adolescent emotionalism, ill health, and the intense religious atmosphere that enveloped her mother and her sister Maria?" Zaturenska says that "When I Am Dead, My Dearest" (1858) gives her the impression of having been conceived in "white heat."[39]

Diane D'Amico in "Christina Rossetti's *Later Life:* The Neglected Sonnet Sequence" in *Victorian Institute Journal* (1980–81), stresses that even in her youth Rossetti feared death. As expressed in *Later Life* (before 1882), the least reviewed of her sonnet sequences, the worst part of death for the dying soul is not only the experience of physical pain, helplessness, and loneliness, but the intense fear that the hoped-for reunion with God will never take place. "Death may indeed prove not only horrifying but totally victorious."[40] As Christina Rossetti wrote in Sonnet 27 of *Later Life:*

> While I supine with ears that cease
>   to hear,
> With eyes that glaze, with heart-
>   pulse running down
> (Alas! no saint rejoicing on her bed),
> May miss the goal at last, may miss
>   a crown.

[82]

Georgina Battiscombe (1981) finds the poet's attitude about death a contrary one—"at one and the same time extraordinarily morbid and unusually joyful." This is exemplified in a pair of sonnets—"Two Thoughts of Death" (1850). The first sonnet reveals the "grisly horror" of death:

> Foul worms fill up her mouth so sweet and red;
> Foul worms are underneath her graceful head; . . .
> These worms are certainly of her flesh.

[298]

But the second reaffirms Rossetti's believe in life everlasting:

> Then my heart answered me:
>   Thou fool, to say
> That she is dead whose night is
>   turned to day;

And no more shall her day turn
back to night.

[299]

Battiscombe says that "For her, death is not to be desired as an escape from this naughty world but as an entry to another and incomparably better one."[41]

The majority of contemporary critics assign more specific causes to such melancholy thoughts; and overwhelmingly they cited unsatisfied longings. Among the poems noted in this context is "Remember" (1849). Here the speaker asks her lover not to forget her when she is dead because that is all he will be able to do for her:

Yet if you should forget me for a while
And afterwards remember, do not grieve;
For if the darkness and corruption leave
A vestige of the thoughts that once I had
Better by far you should forget and smile
Than that you should remember and be sad.

[294]

Another often linked with "Remember" is "Oh Roses for the Flush of Youth" (1849), in which the speaker yearns for an early death:

Oh roses for the flush of youth,
And laurel for the perfect prime;
But pluck an ivy branch for me
Grown old before my time.

[292]

Dolores Rosenblum claims in the spring 1982, issue of *Victorian Poetry* that in Rossetti's works, as well as in those of other Victorian poets, "the myth of suffering for art's sake—Promethean, egoistic, male—is overlaid by the myth of suffering for its own sake—Christian, selfless, female." She notes that the person who suffers in Rossetti's poetry is usually a woman—a cloistered virgin or a betrayed bride waiting patiently and endlessly for her lagging bridegroom; and for this death-in-life woman, "the only resolution is death itself." She dies "because life is not *enough*—and because the aesthetic of renunciation requires this ultimate gesture."[42]

Several critics concerned with the theme of death intertwined with love explain these contrary currents in psychological, and several others in biographical, terms. C. M. Bowra evokes Freud to explain the pairing, saying that in these works "the idea of love turned inexorably to the theme of death, and in this association we can surely see her instinctive shrinking from the surrender which love demands."[43] But Lona Mosk Packer suggests other reasons for what she considers a Freudian death wish in Rossetti's poetry; could the mournful sadness and resignation in her poetry be caused by the realization that she had made a dreadful mistake, that she had bound herself to one man too soon [Collinson], and hence made impossible a rich and satisfying relationship which might have fulfilled her dream of sexual happiness?" Or was her longing for death caused by the lack of earthly love, as seems to be expressed in "Parting After Parting" (1858 and 1864), written after a visit to Scott and his wife in Newcastle?

> Parting after parting,
> Sore loss and gnawing pain:
> Meeting grows half a sorrow
> Because of parting again.
> When shall the day break
> That these things shall not be?
> When shall new earth be ours
> Without a sea,
> And time that is not time
> But eternity.

[200]

These passions, Packer theorizes, were caused by Rossetti's "leaving Scott after having known the rare happiness of sharing a life with him, even temporarily."[44]

The same sadness and wish for death owing to the absence of love, Packer asserts, is expressed in "A Triad" (1856), concerning three women who had had different experiences in love—one shamefully indulges, the second is false and loveless, and the third abstains and negates. They represent, to Packer, the females in Scott's life: the first, Lady Pauline Trevelyan, Scott's mistress; the second, Letitia Norquoy Scott, a wife in name only, a "sluggish wife," soft and smooth as a tinted hyacinth grown in "soulless love;" and the third, Christina Rossetti herself, a virgin "blue with famine after love," finally dying for the lack of it.[45]

Whatever the actual reasons for Rossetti's morbidity, then, most modern critics associate repressed sexuality with the sundering-of-

Portrait of Christina Rossetti. From the oil painting by James Collinson, 1849.

lovers-by-death theme in her poetry, and almost all of them assume that the poet has transferred her emotions to the narrators of
her verses.

Sin and repentance, a theme discerned by many Victorian critics,
is examined by several recent reviewers. Earlier, the focus was
upon *individual* sinners, whereas later it was upon *collective guilt*,
a Jungian view of the individual personality as product and recep-
tacle of its ancestral history. One poem that undergoes such analysis is "Eve" (1865):

> 'I, Eve, sad mother
> Of all who must live,
> I, not another,
> Plucked bitterest fruit to give
> My friend, husband, lover.
> O wanton eyes, run over!
> Who but I should grieve?
> Cain hath slain his brother:
> Of all who must die, mother,
> Miserable Eve!'

[373]

Contemporary critic Nesca A. Robb points out that since Rossetti believed that every soul is made in the image of God and
tainted by the Fall, Eve's guilt is reflected in every soul. Thus, "in
Christina's version, sorrow-ful and penetrating as Eve's own, we
are all fratricides in the wrongs we do each other, since all are
wrongs done to the love in which we are brothers." To Eve, she
says, "Every cruelty, every falsehood, strikes at something that is
yet common to us all." Robb contends that the crime of murder,
particularly fratricide, was always vivid in Rossetti's imagination
because she had such tender affections for her own brothers.[46]

Bowra, too, sees that to Rossetti "the fall of man was a fearful
reality, not to be shirked or explained away, but a permanent
source of shame and sorrow." He believes that the poet supplied
Eve with her own guilt feelings—Eve, the original sinner, whose
sins have been transmitted to all generations. For Bowra "Eve" is
effective "because of the passionate conviction which Christina
puts into it, and becomes a symbol of all men and women who
understand that the evil of the world is their own fault."[47]

Several modern critics of Rossetti, in agreement with Daiches
that "perhaps more fruitful than general psychological and
psychoanalytic theories of the origin of art are the particular appli-

cations to particular cases,"[48] address such theories to particular
poems, hoping to uncover the ways in which the poet's imagination operated under certain conditions. They are concerned with
the poet's emotional conflicts, which elicit interpretations of individual works. For example, F. L. Lucas writes in *Ten Victorian
Poets* of a split in Rossetti's psyche—a conflict between "the frail
yet indomitable young saint of Mary Virgin and of the Annuncia-
tion" and her alter ego, "the more human, humourous Christina
who loved children, and furry wombats, and the calling of gay
Goblin-men from twilit market of forbidden things." She notes
that sometimes "the meek nun's veil is flung aside and from these
lips of Christian modesty breaks the proud and angry cry of some
pagan Medea!" Then Rossetti suddenly turns "to throw her misery, contemptuous of man, at the feet of God,"[49] as in this verse of
"The Heart Knoweth Its Own Bitterness" (1857):

> Not in this world of hope deferred,
>   This world of perishable stuff;
> Eye hath not seen or ear hath heard
>   Nor heart conceived that full "enough":
> Here moans the separating sea,
>   Here harvests fail, here breaks the heart:
>   There God shall join and no man part,
> I full of Christ and Christ of me.
>
> [192–93]

K. E. Janowitz, writing in *Victorian Poetry* for December 14,
1973, sees another split in Rossetti's psyche—a conflict between
expectation and despondency—in the poem "Three Stages" (1854)
[called "Restive" in manuscript]. He suggests that "the poet-
speaker imagines herself to have given up the will to live":

> I thought to deal with the death-stroke
>   at a blow:
> To give all, once for all, but never
>   more:—
>
> [289]

Rossetti means to be ambiguous in these lines, Janowitz says:
"Does 'To give all' imply the exercise of will in the form of an
action, . . . Or should the phrase . . . be taken in a passive sense, as
a self-surrendering act?" The final lines—

I may pursue, and yet may not attain,
Athirst and panting all the days I
    live:
Or seem to hold, yet nerve myself to
    give
What once I gave, again.

[290]

—"parallel the poem's opening lines." But if the meaning is equivocal, he says, "we are left finally with the image of a perpetual internal struggle between the antipodes of hope and despair."[50]

For Lona Mosk Packer, "Three Nuns" (1849–50), a dramatic monologue dealing with the emotional experience of three women who had chosen to become brides of Christ, calls up not two but *three* sides of Rossetti's nature—the poetic, the erotic, and the religious. Always Rossetti "was to reveal one of these three facets of her personality in her poetry, often all simultaneously, and sometimes in warring conflict."[51]

Swann finds that Rossetti's "autobiographical" ghosts and wretched "ghostscapes are often symbolic of Christina's state of mind, and that the ghosts may represent her own tormented self, or forces or people which have brought her pain." Witness "A Chilly Night" (1856), where, Swann notes, "Christina wants only to join her mother in ghostland":[52]

I called: 'O my Mother dear,'—
I sobbed: 'O my Mother kind,
Make a lonely bed for me
And shelter it from the wind.

[321]

"Goblin Market" is the poem most often used by the moderns as a vehicle for showing what their chosen psychological system(s) can do to relate such disparate elements as tugs-of-war, phases of personality, dream and reality. In fact, Conrad Daniel Festa asserts in his dissertation on Rossetti prepared at the University of South Carolina (1969), "if any of [Rossetti's] poems can be said to emerge fresh from her unconscious mind, molded only by her imagination, 'Goblin Market' is that poem." It is, he feels, an expression of her desires, fears, and beliefs, "freed from the censor in her conscious mind."[53]

Martine Watson Brownley, writing in the Spring 1969, issue of *Essays in Literature,* takes a similar view: In "Goblin Market,"

Rossetti is consciously examining "certain psychological and emotional states," employing the sisters' experiences with the goblins as "symbolic terms for her portrayal of a feminine initiation into adult sexuality." Lizzie stands for mature love—"a love that gives." She triumphs over the animalistic goblins who represent a selfish love—"a love that takes, that requires sacrifice of personal essence" because she "embodies an alternative to narcissistic, sensual sexuality, a selfless love which knows the proper relationship of the physical and the spiritual." This is the only work in which Rossetti "leashed powerful psychic forces in compelling metaphors"; and, indeed, she never treated such forces again: "The woman who pasted pieces of paper over the more explicit lines in Swinburne's poetry could never have faced the actual implications of the stunningly effective parable of human sexuality which somehow welled up from her unconscious self"[54] in this unforgettable poem.

Ellen Moers, author of *Literary Women* (1976), believes that "Goblin Market" not only developed the two-sisters theme that Rossetti handles with "particular intensity" and "hissing vigor"—vide the poet's use of sisters as "symbolic oppositions" in other poems, such as "Noble Sisters" (1860) and "Sister Maude" (1860), wherein the siblings are "rivals in love or hostile to each other's passion"[55]—but is as well an erotic Gothic fantasy—"perverse and also realistic." To many middle-class intellectual women, "the rough and tumble sexuality of the nursery . . . was the only heterosexual world that Victorian literary spinsters were ever freely and physically to explore." Moers recalls Freud's lecture on symbols, the claim that the small animals often present in dreams may symbolize little brothers and sisters. Rossetti, through her experience with her siblings, surely "had access through fantasies derived from the night side of the Victorian nursery—a world where childish cruelty and childish sexuality come to the fore."[56] The brother-monsters tempt and harass the sisters with a twofold purpose: to intoxicate and to torture and destroy them with forbidden fruit. Laura, the weaker sister, succumbs to the tempters; Lizzie, the stronger one, resists eating the fruit although she is cruelly mauled and smeared with the juices. Witness Lizzie offering herself physically to Laura after her experience with the goblins:

> 'Did you miss me?
> Come and kiss me.
> Never mind my bruises,

> Hug me, kiss me, suck my juices . . .
> Eat me, drink me, love me; . . .'

[7]

Moers notes that the verb "suck," to suggest a sensation with "mixed lust and pain," is used "to an extreme that must be called perverse." When Laura reacts—"She kissed and kissed her with a hungry mouth"—"it is the most erotic movement in the poem." Moers does not imply "that *Goblin Market* belongs to the history of pornography as a Victorian celebration of oral sex, but that Christina Rossetti wrote a poem unconsciously . . . about the erotic life of children."[57]

An anonymous editorial voice in the September 1973, issue of *Playboy*, offering "Entertainment for Men," does claim pornographic status for "Goblin Market": "Hiding between the lines of this nice Victorian nursery tale lurk monsters from the Freudian night"; the poem "might be called the all-time hard-core pornographic classic for tiny tots."[58] Accompanying the editorial matter are drawings—erotic to some, lurid to others—that interpret the narrative-verse.

Georgina Battiscombe, in her 1981 volume, calls "Goblin Market" inescapably erotic. "Even small children too young to be aware of sex," she claims, "sometimes find themselves, for no reason that they understand or explain, obscurely puzzled and embarrassed by the poem." Although consciously Rossetti may have recalled her father's representation of herself and Maria as "lovely turtle-doves in the nest of love," the "sexual undertones in *Goblin Market* are fairly obvious": the two sisters "Cheek to cheek and breast to breast / Locked together in one nest," can have symbolized in Rossetti's subconscious mind "an unconscious piece of eroticism." And yet, says Battiscombe, "if the sexual interpretation throws some light on Christina's subconscious mind the Christian one is closer to her conscious thought." Surely, Lizzie, braving the sadistic attacks of the goblins to save her sister, is a parallel to Christ, who willingly faced temptation, suffering, and death to save mankind.[59]

Still other critics believe that the two girls in "Goblin Market" are *unconscious* representatives of different sides of the self. For Ellen Golub, in the 1975 issue of *Literature and Psychology*, an American quarterly of literary criticism, "as informed by depth psychology," they represent the two halves of the divided self; the split is healed at the end of the poem, when Lizzie passes on the fruit juices to Laura and saves her life.[60]

To A. A. De Vitis, a contributor to the Spring 1968 issue of *The Journal of Popular Culture,* which examines trends in literature and the arts, the two sisters are the embodiments of the two sides of the artist's character: "Laura is the passionate artist who would drink too deep and too fully from the fountain of experience; Lizzie is the obedient maiden who fears to venture far from the safe anchorage of hearth, home, and religion." Although Rossetti herself disclaimed any allegorical content in the poem, De Vitis asserts that the poem is more than a delightful fairy tale with portentous implications of evil and sorcery:

> Christina may have been attempting to divert attention from some hidden meaning by disclaiming any conscious effort at allegory; perhaps some of the passages of the poem embarrassed her, because with time she came to appreciate their erotic and psychological importunities; maybe she might at first have been totally unaware of any implications in the poem.[61]

He adds that Rossetti's manner of indicating the conflict in the creative personality illustrates her belief that the artist "must come face to face with the reality of evil, and by confronting defeat it."[62]

Sandra M. Gilbert and Susan Gubar in *The Madwoman in the Attic: The Woman Writer and the Nineteenth-Century Literary Imagination* (1979) assert that "Goblin Market" has "a tantalizing number of . . . meanings about and for women in particular." Laura—like Eve—engorging the fruit is "enacting an affirmation of intellectual (or poetic) as well as sexual selfhood." Both women seem to be "metaphorically eating *words* and enjoying the taste of power." But, in their quest for power, Eve, Laura—and Rossetti herself—are overcome with guilt and their aspirations can only be partaken furtively. The poem, the coauthors say, implies that "genius and sexuality *are* diseases in women"—diseases suggesting madness and barrenness, signifying Jeanie's and Laura's alienation from "their own healthful, child-oriented female sexuality" and their Victorian "socially ordained roles as 'modest maidens': participating in domestic chores." To Gilbert-Gubar, the haunted glen is more than a female sex symbol; "it represents a chasm in the mind," the goblins being "the desirous little creatures so many women writers [unconsciously] have recorded encountering in the haunted glens of their own minds, hurrying scurrying furry ratlike *its* or *ids,* inescapable *incubi.*" The edibles symbolize the "honey-sweet fruit of art, fruit that is analogous to (or identical with) the lucious fruit of self-gratifying sensual pleasure."[63]

For Stephen Prickett, writing in *Victorian Fantasy* (1979), how-ever, the expressions of alienation in "Goblin Market" are non-gender-specific. The poem is a fantasy of "a divided mind," of a "divided society" as well, each too frightened "to come to terms with its own deepest needs and desires." The fairy men are "gob-lins of the mind," offering "a surrogate language of sexuality," and woe betide those who disregard them.[64]

Maureen Duffy, writing in *The Erotic World of Faery* (1972), says that Rossetti, like other artists of her era, had a penchant for the "grotesquerie of the erotic;" "Goblin Market" is both gro-tesque and erotic. Laura and Lizzie represent a "double female image, . . . an interesting component of the period's eroticism akin to the heterosexual male desire to see blue films about lesbians." The vision of the two women embracing.

> Cheek to cheek and breast to breast
> Locked together in one nest.
>
> [3]

offers "duplicate feminine images ripe for polygamy." The goblins, representing "animal instincts, promote their fruit, symbolizing premarital sex; the curl Laura pays them with represents pubic hair, and her gorging of the fruit "is a powerful masturbatory fantasy of feeding at the breast." Hence, Laura's reaction after she "sucked" the fruit resembles "the contemporary classic description of the habitual masturbator." The goblins' attempt to press the fruit into Lizzie's mouth "suggests attempted rape," and Laura's emotional kissing of her sister after Lizzie's return "is a violent image of spontaneous orgasm." Thus, to Duffy, the goblins repre-sent not actual but "fantasy sex." But for each sister, the tempta-tion is different:

> Contemplating her sister's aroused eroticism (since they shared the same bed she could hardly avoid it), rouses Lizzie's sexual curiosity but she resists. Laura is able to slake hers on her sister and her affection for her, not surprisingly since Lizzie will be the image of her mother, and so fulfil her homosexual fantasy.[65]

Germaine Greer finds "Goblin Market" a deeply perverse poem" whose secret is known to Rossetti alone. Homosexuals, Greer says, will argue that the poem lauds physical love between sisters, and those who view heterosex as perverted and cruel will assent. However, we have all "grown up with the unexpressed incest taboo which regulated the degree of physical contact we think appropriate between brothers and sisters, and all of us have somehow violated it." She believes the poem "is about guilt, and the pleasure of guilt," leaving us "with the overriding fact of its subtle perversity and our own complicity."[66] Yet, she claims that "even the most unashamed of post-Freudian readers" are reluctant to fully interpret the plot "for fear that to unravel it would be to reveal more of the psychology of the unraveler than it would of the meaning of the poem itself."[67]

C. J. Jung's contention that "mankind has never lacked powerful images to lend magical aid against all the uncanny things that live in the depths of the psyche"[68] has led to the modern critics' more complex search for universal archetypical images and symbols in literature, and Rossetti's critics are among them. For example, Conrad Festa in *English Language Notes* for September 1973, calls attention to the three symbols in the first stanza of "A Birthday" (1857—a bird, an apple tree, and a shell—which he regards as fertility symbols, expressive of "full, open, and complete joy for love's fulfillment, or expected fulfillment." The bird in the poem is symbolic of a soul, Festa contends, recalling that in fairy tales the bird symbolizes love yearnings; in myths the bird is frequently the transformation of the lover. The bird's nest is in a "watered shoot"—that is, according to Festa, a pool or fountain—"symbols of fulfillment used by individuals whose lives are inhibited or dried up."[69]

He finds the tree in "A Birthday" to be a "clearly archetypal" symbol, and notes that Sir James George Frazer stated in *The Golden Bough* that among primitive cultures the tree represented all of animate nature and, in particular, man himself. What is more, says Festa, Jung calls the shell ["My heart is like a rainbow shell"] a major fertility symbol associated with water by thirsty travelers and pilgrims, recorded in medieval allegories as a symbol of physical refreshment.

The symbols in the second stanza, Festa continues, are "clearly related to Christian culture and thought." The birds in this stanza are particularized—importantly, a dove, which "traditionally represents the abiding spirit of God." The peacock represents "His eternal and omniscient nature," and the grapes and vine are "the 'People of Israel,' Christ's chosen people who are to inhabit the Kingdom of Heaven." The lily and the pomegranate are familiar symbols of spring, fertility, and rebirth, and suggest eternal life and joy. And all Christian symbols in the poem suggest "Rossetti's death and resurrection, that new birth into eternal life and royal marriage of eternal union with the Savior."[70]

Several of Rossetti's modern critics assert that "Goblin Market" is, on one level, a didactic version of the Edenic myth. For Marian Shalkhauser in the Autumn 1956 issue of the American publication *Victorian Newsletter*, "Goblin Market" is a "unique fairy tale in which a feminine cast of characters is substituted for the masculine cast of the Biblical sin-redemption sequence." Lizzie, the pure sister, is the "symbol of Christ; Laura represents Adam-Eve and consequently all of sinful mankind."[71]

Gilbert-Gubar claim that, consciously or semiconsciously, the purpose of "Goblin Market" is "sexual/religious." Wicked men, like the evil Satan, offer Laura sensuous forbidden fruits in exchange for a golden curl, symbolic of "permission to 'rape' a lock of her hair." When she succumbs to their demands—signifying her loss of virginity—the goblins have no further desire for her and she goes into a "conventional Victorian decline," becoming an old, gray, witchlike woman. The analogy, say Gilbert-Gubar, is similar to Eve's having to leave Eden and entering "the realm of generation." But,

> just as Christ intervened to save mankind by offering his body and blood as bread and wine for general spiritual consumption, so Laura's "good" sister Lizzie, like a Female savior, negotiates with the goblins (as Christ did with Satan) and offers herself to be eaten and drunk in a womanly holy communion. And just as Christ redeemed mankind from Original Sin, restoring at least the possibility of heaven to Eve's descendants, so Lizzie rehabilitates Laura, changing her back from a lost witch to a virginal bride and ultimately leading her into a heaven of innocent domesticity.[72]

Beyond this didacticism, however, Rossetti betrays a note of *unconscious* nostalgia, say Gilbert-Gubar, as Laura, now "a true Victorian angel-in-the-house," recalls "those pleasant days long gone / Of not returning time," in the "haunted glen" with the "wicked quaint fruit-merchant men."

However, it is Cora Kaplan's claim in her essay on Christina Rossetti and Emily Dickinson that "Goblin Market" is not a recapitulation of Eve's fall. The difference, she says, is that "while the snake's apple produces sensations of shame in the Edenic couple, the goblins' fruit gives Laura knowledge of desire but not shame." Then, too, Laura and Lizzie are sisters, not mates; hence "the deliberate contrast which Rossetti establishes between her fairy tale and the Edenic myth."[73]

Still another Jungian theory, set out in *Psyche and Symbol* (1958), finds the dream the most important approach to the unconscious. If, for Freud, every dream offers vicarious fulfillment of a repressed desire—usually related to infantile sexuality—for Jung, dreams give expression to unconscious fears as well as to wishes. Jung, however, did not stop here. Departing from Freud's conceptions, Liliane Frey-Rohn has written in *From Freud to Jung: A Comparative Study of the Psychology of the Unconscious* (1974), "Jung found it necessary to go back into the archaic levels of the psyche, and in this manner to establish contact with the image-creating aspect of the unconscious, that is, the original meanings and primal images."[74] He theorized that since primordal images and instincts are preformed in the brain of every individual, man's collective unconscious inherits the patterns of life and behavior from his ancestors.[75]

This Jungian approach has influenced several contemporary critics of Rossetti, among them Nesca Robb, who asserts that each person has had an Edenic moment—the life of innocent sensuousness and unrest of the spirit of childhood. In *Four in Exile,* she contends that the Adam-Even experience is repeated over and over in Rossetti's works. For example, the "Paradise that haunts her dreams" in "Long Barren" (1856) "is the glorified image of the natural Eden of her childhood."[76] It is a paradise "doubly lost" because the poet realizes that the kingdom of the spirit is irrevocably closed to the adult; and nothing can open it "except another kingdom whose beauty lightens us but rarely, and in glimpses soon to be obscure":[77]

> Thou Rose of Sharon, Cedar of broad roots,
> Vine of sweet fruits,
> Thou Lily of the vale with fadeless leaf,
> Of thousands Chief,
> Feed thou my feeble shoots.

[246]

Nature's loveliness, for Rossetti, is short-lived, says Robb: "Beauty, health, pleasure, worldly greatness, vanish like smoke. . . . The hopes of youth and the experience of a lifetime pass both alike into oblivion."[78] Among the other poems Robb examines in this light are "Gone for Ever" (1846) and "Shut Out" (1856).

"To remain in that young ecstasy one must never wake," Robb continues, as seems to be the inference too of "Dream-Love" (1854):

> Young Love lies dreaming
>   Till summer days are gone,—
> Dreaming and drowsing
>   Away to perfect sleep:
> He sees the beauty
>   Sun hath not looked upon
> And tastes the fountain
>   Unutterably deep.
>
>   [312]

For Rossetti, the central human tragedy is that we do not appreciate the days of childhood until they have been taken from us forever. Thus "Sooner or later we repeat the experience of our first parents."[79]

But Georgina Battiscombe, in yet another piece—this a contribution to *British Writers: Elizabeth Gaskell and Francis Thompson*, volume 5 (1982)—entertains no such notion. Although Rossetti certainly loved childhood, the poet never did look back to a childhood Eden: "Her gaze is always forward toward . . . the city that can only be entered through the gate of death. Heaven, and no other, is the country of her poetic imagining," as we read in "Mother Country" (1866):[80]

> Oh what is that country
>   And where can it be,
> Not mine own country,
>   But dearer far to me?
> Yet mine own country,
>   If I one day may see
> Its gold and ivory.
> As I lie dreaming,
>   It rises, that land;
> There rises before me
>   Its green golden strand,
> With the bowing cedars
>   And the shining sand;
> It sparkles and flashes
>   Like a shaken brand.
>
>   [245]

Still other psychological criticism is informed by the four archetypes designated by Jung in developing his theories of individua-
tion: the shadow—the inferior or negative part of the personality,
unconsciously repressed; the persona—the mask man adopts to
meet the demands of social convention; and the anima—the compensatory female side of man's personality—with its counterpart,
the animus—the compensatory masculine side of woman's personality. Both man and woman constantly search for wholeness, com-
pletion, and rebirth.

Among the critics evaluating Rossetti's poetry in this light is
Winston Weathers, who notes in *Victorian Poetry* for Spring 1965,
that Rossetti's whole psychological life has been one of withdrawal
and, further, "that our personalities are subject to an analysis into
parts." The fragmented personality in "A Triad" (1856) thus reveals
Rossetti's own character—the poet's tripartite division of self.
(Packer too, it will be remembered, sees a tripartite division of
character in the poem but assumes these to be the women in William Bell Scott's life.) On the surface, says Weathers, the poem is
obviously a simple discussion of love itself; "on its mythic level it
presents an analysis of the self again into its various psychological
states." The three maidens "represent the fragmentation of self,"[81]
without any integration of resolution:

> One shamed herself in love; one temperately
> 　Grew gross in soulless love, a sluggish wife
> One famished died for love. Thus two of three
> 　Took death for love and won him after strife.
> One droned in sweetness like a fattened bee:
> 　All on the threshold, yet all short of life.
>
> 　　　　　　　　　　　　　　　　　　[329]

With regard to "Goblin Market," Weathers contends, the underlying drama is in the tension between the "eternal polarities of self,
the one, the Dionysian [Laura], leading to tragedy, the other, the
Apollonian [Lizzie], leading to survival." The poem is simply
"Rossetti's discussion of psychological truths which she witnessed
in herself and which are universally significant."[82]

Weathers asserts that in "Maiden-Song" (1863), too, Rossetti is
"sketching allegorically the struggle for psychological integration." Although the work has other concerns—religious and even
mystical experience and the relationship of that experience to
self—"one of the major motifs in her mythic fabric is that of the
fragmented self moving or struggling toward harmony and bal-

ance." But unlike the unresolved fragmentation of "A Triad," there is a perfect resolution at the end of "Maiden-Song"; it is, in fact, "a little fable of integration." At first, the three sisters—tall Meggan, dainty May, and fair Margaret—separate. The conflict, Weathers tells us, is that both Meggan and May accept lovers to escape from their sister Margaret. But Margaret, realizing the "incipient separation and fragmentation of self," lifts her voice and sings, bringing a king to her door not only to love her but, more important, to lead her sisters home. Thus Weathers believes that "we should read Christina Rossetti as a serious masterful eschatological and psychological poet who records in her poetry universal and timeless human experiences."[83]

Dolores Rosenblum asserts in *Victorian Poetry* for Spring 1982, that Rossetti's religious poetry adopts "a timeless background and ritualized pattern for self-abnegation" to transcend the aesthetic of emotional suffering:

> By becoming "witness" as well as "model," the vigil-keeper as well as the dead person, Rossetti overcomes the despair inherent in the renunciatory pose. Ultimately, by exploring the possibilities of compassionate "looking," Rossetti transforms the witness's isolated gazing into a collective act: the vigil—and valediction—for the dead.

Rossetti's religious poetry, says Rosenblum, "not only registers her alienation, but also achieves, by 'looking,' integration and community."[84]

One perduring interest of the critics since the Victorian era has been to assign Rossetti's verses to an artistic tradition. But contemporary critics are less apt than those of the 1900–1939 period to compare Rossetti with Victorian women poets; several compare her with the religious poets of all centuries as well as with her secular contemporaries of both sexes. An American, Hoxie Neal Fairchild, for example, the author of *Religious Trends in English Poetry, 1830–1899* (1966), believes that Rossetti "is the most accomplished orthodox Christian writer of authentic poetry between Vaughan and Hopkins."[85]

Nesca Robb finds that Rossetti has much in common with George Herbert, Henry Vaughan, and John Donne in sentiment and source of inspiration. "The Bible is her mind's daily bread. The use of Biblical phrases and allusions has become for her, as it had for those seventeenth century Christians, the use of an instinctive second language."[86]

But Molly Mahood argues in *Poetry and Humanism* (1950) that although Rossetti has much in common with Herbert—the theme of renunciation and the use of an imagined dialogue between the speaker and the Deity—she lacks the "audacity, actuality, humour . . . of Herbert's unshakeable theocentric faith."[87]

Germaine Greer notes that Rossetti is included in the tradition of English religious poetry but claims that "if she is a religious poet, . . . her religion is a matter of devout sentiment rather than an intellectual apprehension of the nature of God or any mystical intimation of communion with Him." Rather, her piety was "a metaphor for her own frustrated sexuality." Therefore, she is similar to "the lesser religious ladies who penned nonsensical hymns in the nineteenth century."[88]

Marya Zaturenska asserts, however, that Rossetti's verses are more sincerely religious than "the persistent note of unconvincing religiosity in most of the women poets who preceded her—Letitia Landon, Felicia Hemans, Elizabeth Browning, or the equally feeble but deeply devout Adelaide Proctor. . . . Beside her even her truly religious younger contemporary, Alice Meynell, seems too literary, too mannered, almost affected."[89] Sometimes, says Zaturenska, in her distraught moments of "self-doubt and pain, Rossetti opened her heart to God in accents as painful as those of Gerard Manley Hopkins in his sonnets."[90]

F. L. Lucas contends that although Rossetti would have been happier unborn, she is the best of all the English poets. Her work is a perfect counterpart to her brother's—"beside his heady wine, her cup of pure cold water; beside his organ roll, her silver vesper-bell; beside his Blessed Damozel, this Damozel to the end unblest."[91]

According to Nesca Robb, Christina Rossetti is indebted to the Pre-Raphaelites for the "ornate archaism" and the "sensuous element—image, description, technical device . . . always, as it were, the body of the spiritual."[92] Jerome H. Buckley, author of *The Pre-Raphaelites* (1968), states that Christina Rossetti "was from the beginning both close to the center of the Pre-Raphaelite movement and at the same time, in her quiet asceticism, aloof from bohemian influence."[93] Christian Murciaux, a critic for *Révue de Paris* (December 1964), also finds Rossetti's poems mirroring the style and aims of the Pre-Raphaelites, with whom she was associated.[94] Marya Zaturenska believes that in "A Birthday" (1857)—"surely one of the happiest expressions of lyrical emotion in the language—we find the purest essence of the Pre-Raphaelite ideal":[95]

> Raise me a dais of silk and down;
>> Hang it with vair and purple dyes; . . .

[335]

Georgina Battiscombe (1965) writes that Rossetti's poems are "as full of colour and detail as a Pre-Raphaelite picture: she crams them with jewels and flowers, with rich stuffs and tapestries, with beautiful things to see and touch and smell and taste,"[96] offering as an example these lines of "A Birthday":

> Carve it in doves and pomegranates,
>> And peacocks with a hundred eyes;
> Work it in gold and silver grapes,
>> In leaves and silver fleurs-de-lys;

[335]

But Bowra maintains that only "one side of [Christina Rossetti] was Pre-Raphaelite, fond of pictorial effects and unusual images, capable of telling a story with a proper sense of its dramatic possibilities." The other side of the poet was "a truly Romantic temperament, trained to look for beauty in mysterious realms of experience, and able to find it without any strain of forcing of herself."[97]

Swann finds Christina Rossetti sharing with her famous and versatile brother, Dante Gabriel, a penchant for medievalism, supernaturalism, and sensuous imagery. But "in one all-important element she was unlike him and the Pre-Raphaelites: in her command of whimsy." To Swann, "whimsy or that which is odd, quaint, and perversely charming" is the very source of the power in Rossetti's fantastic poems, and the element that separates her from the Pre-Raphaelites.[98]

Rather than place the aggregate of Rossetti's poetry in a tradition, some contemporary critics render judgment on *particular* works. For example, in the Spring 1972, issue of *Victorian Newsletter*, Warren Herendeen detects a similarity in the temptation theme and the use of the supernatural in "Goblin Market" and Shakespeare's *A Midsummer Night's Dream* but notes the differences in the treatment of women in these works: "Shakespeare's girls are very alike in nature and very different in appearance. Christina Rossetti's girls are look-alikes but their natures differ."[99]

In the Spring 1972, issue of *Seventeenth Century News*, Herendeen makes a comparison between Rossetti's "Goblin Market" and two of Andrew Marvell's poems, "The Garden" and "Bermudas":

"The poetess may seem a fantastic visitor to Marvell's tranquil climes, but reflection reveals that poet and poetess are sectaries of one communion. The active and contemplate lives cross in these two religious poetic conceptions of the true garden of the soul."[100]

Gilbert-Gubar see a resemblance between Rossetti's goblin men in "Goblin Market" and John Keat's "belle dame" in "La Belle Dame Sans Merci." Both poems, they say, symbolize "the relationship of poetry and starvation to an encounter with interior otherness incarnated in a magical being of the opposite sex." Keats's knight was deserted by the lady in the meads after he wooed her, as was Laura after her encounter with the goblins in their wooded haunt, and both abandoned lovers starved and lost their vitality after their betrayal. "Yet in Keats's case, . . . the poet's abandonment is only temporary, no matter what the knight's fate might be," while Laura/Rossetti is persuaded "that her original desire to eat the forbidden fruit of art was a vain and criminal impulse."[101]

Diane D'Amico, writing in the Summer 1981 *Victorian Poetry* detects the influence in Rossetti's early poetry of the themes of Maturin's ill-fated lovers: The passionate women in his novels spoke in a language that appealed to the poet's own strong-willed nature—a yearning for both heaven and earth. "In this language she could begin to examine the suffering of the isolated self, the necessity of choosing, and the hope of the soul's salvation, gradually finding for such spiritual concerns her own poetic voice."[102] In fact, says D'Amico, Maturin's *Melmoth The Wanderer* must have inspired "Isadora" (1847), a dramatic monologue:

> I have conquered; it is done,
>   Yea the death-struggle is o'er,
> And the hopeless quiet won:—
>   I shall see his face no more:—
>
> . . . .
>   Blessed Saviour, take my soul
> To thy Paradise and care:—
> Paradise, will he be there?
>
> [106–7]

If today's critics are more wont than previously to be gender blind when comparing Rossetti's works with those of other poets, it is also true—and particularly in the last ten years—that critics have been paying greater attention to Rossetti's portrayal of women and their social role. For Annis Pratt, discussing "The

New Feminist Criticism" in general in *College English* for May 1971, such critics are concerned not only with "*textual analysis* to determine which works are . . . successful, but also a *contextual analysis* which considers the relevance of a group of works, even if artistically flawed, as a reflection of the situation of women"[103]

For Miriam Sagan, writing in the 1980 issue of the *Pre-Raphaelite Review* and addressing Christina Rossetti's works in particular, this is "a new form of criticism," and "its tenets are often embryonic or unclear." But it does bring to light the historical problems encountered by women writers and helps to define the female sensibility. Literary critics working in this vein, she notes, "had to devise new critical approaches" to Rossetti's work[104]—witness the multifarious sexual, psychological, and social analyses of "Goblin Market" by feminist critics.

Recognition of Christina Rossetti as a woman of her own times, subject to its conventions and at home in them is well illustrated in Marya Zaturenska's response, in her 1949 work, to the Victorian critic Andrew Lang's eulogy of Rossetti at her death. Lang's "there can be little doubt that we are now deprived of the greatest English poet of her sex, which is made to inspire poetry rather than to create it," is something Zaturenska finds "intolerable." But she adds: "Since Christina was not a feminist, no doubt she would have accepted this intolerable praise with proper humility."[105]

The poet was at home in her society—but not above poking fun at its women—according to Swann in *Wonder and Whimsy*. In such nursery rhymes as "Freaks of Fashion" (circa 1878), he says, the poet was given to satirizing lightly the society of mid-Victorian English women who made a fuss over their costumes, an interest which the somberly dressed Rossetti found ridiculous.[106]

> Flushing salmon, flushing sulphur
>   Haughty Cockatoos
> Answer—'Hoods may do for mornings,
>   But for evenings choose
> High head-dresses, curved like crescents
>   Such as well-bred persons use.'

[396]

And he sees her taking "a sly glance at Victorian prudery (and perhaps her own, which led her to paste paper over the franker passages in Swinburne's poetry) as the parent-birds are advising their children what to wear."[107]

> Here a rustling and a whirring,
>   As of fans outspread,
> Hinted that mammas felt anxious
>   Lest the next thing said
> Might prove less than quite judicious,
>   or even underbred.
>
> [396]

If not a feminist, what was Christina Rossetti's attitude toward women? Did she herself perpetuate the view of women that Simone de Beauvoir has characterized in *The Second Sex* (1971) as "the hostile Other"? Take "Eve" (1865), for instance;

> 'While I sit at the door,
> Sick to gaze within,
> Mine eye weepeth sore
> For sorrow and sin:
> As a tree my sin stands
> To darken all lands;
> Death is the fruit it bore.'
>
> [373]

Nesca Robb, however, finds Rossetti unwilling to assume the role of Eve-the-corrupter. Robb asserts that Rossetti certainly makes clear in "The Convent Threshold" (1858) that the lovers must expiate their faults equally because "Their shared sin demands a shared repentance if its consequences are not to pursue them hereafter:"

> I seek the spot of glass and fire
> To wash the spot, to burn the snare;
> Lo, stairs are meant to lift us higher:
> Mount with me, mount the kindled
>   stair.
>
> [340]

Although the speaker hopes that she may be saved by her renunciation of earthly happiness and be admitted into heaven, says Robb, "she will always be shorn of her full stature even there, if the one who was part of her life for good and evil will not, through penitence be made whole with her."[108]

Lona Mosk Packer claims that Rossetti reveals a psychologically curious attitude toward the respective functions of man and woman—"The concept of the maimed male as the carrier of death in the genetic process, with his partner, the living mother, spared for the sorrow of childbearing." Then "are we to assume that Christina considered the female the stable and enduring spiritual element, source of spiritual as well as of physical life, whereas the expendable male represents the mortal and perishable elements?"[109]

Of the heroine Lizzie's victory over the goblins in "Goblin Market," Ellen Golub states: "such a poetic exercise might have granted the vicarious experience of mastery which was a rare commodity for the Victorian woman in her limited social sphere."[110]

Ellen Moers offers the opinion in *Literary Women* (1976) that "nothing separates female experience from male experience more sharply, and more early in life than the compulsion to visualize the self." Rossetti signals this in "A Royal Princess" (1861):

> All my walls are lost in mirrors,
>   whereupon I trace
> Self to right hand, self to left hand,
>   self in every place,
> Self-same solitary figure, self-same
>   seeking face.

[35]

Moers reasons that, from infancy, a girl's appearance is scrutinized ruthlessly by everyone, particularly women, and above all by her own mother. "The savagery of girlhood accounts in part for . . . the self-disgust, the self-hatred, and the impetus to self-destruction. . . ." Despair does not belong to the female or male sex or class; "but to give *visual* form to the feat of self, to hold anxiety up to the Gothic mirror of the imagination, may well be more common in the writings of women than of men."[111]

Moers further notes that women's love poetry is different from men's: "Women's love poetry seems to be I-You poetry, not I-He poetry on the whole."[112] They write directly to their lovers, not about their lovers, thus attaining a more realistic result because "the lover seems to be a real man, because he is You." Women poets do not bemoan the poisonous effect of love; rather, they exult in love, as does Rossetti in Sonnet 1 of her sonnet sequence *Monna Innominata* (before 1882):

> Come back to me, who wait and
>   watch for you:
> Or come not yet, for it is over then,

                    And long it is before you come
                        again,
                    So far between my pleasures are and
                        few.

[58–59]

   Some feminist critics maintain that Rossetti expressed in her
poetry dissatisfaction with the role assigned to women. For example, Barbara Fass, writing in the Spring 1976, issue of *Victorian
Poetry,* notes that although Rossetti's "few recorded words on the
feminist movement in her own era [as in Sonnet 5 of the *Monna
Innominata* sonnets: ". . . woman is the helpmeet made for man"
(60)] show her to be antipathetic toward it, her early poem
["Repining" (1847)] reveals her sharp awareness of woman's
uniquely passive and monotonous life, her dependence upon man
to rescue her from an almost existential nothingness." The speaker
in the poem is unhappy at "a task not only monotonous and
lonely, but typically female and confining so that her only hope lies
in a man who will rescue her from such solitary tedium":

                    She sat always through the long day
                    Spinning the weary thread away;
                    And ever said in undertone,
                    'Come, that I be no more alone.'

[9]

   This attitude, Fass says, is similar to Madeline's in Keats's "The
Eve of St. Agnes" in both poets'"ambiguous use of 'love' as a
bridge between the secular and the religious." But Fass notes in
Rossetti's poem an intimation that religion was also "a refuge from
some deeper psychic conflict and provided the haven into which
she could escape from the relationship she seemed so much in her
poetry to seek."[113]
   In "The Prince's Progress" (1861–65), as in "Repining," a
woman awaits a tardy lover's return. Here handmaidens give advice on how to pass the time away:

                    'How long shall I wait, come heat
                        come rime?'
                    'Till the strong Prince comes, who
                        must come in time'
                    (Her women say); 'there's a moun-

tain to climb,
A river to ford. Sleep, dream and
     sleep;
Sleep' (they say): 'we've muffled
     the chime;
Better dream than weep.'

[26]

Fass notes the marked contrast consciously drawn by the poet "between woman's passive and man's active life." It is the Prince who journeys, who loves, who acts, who can encounter a variety of experience, and "Christina Rossetti may have welcomed this chance to share vicariously in his adventures."[114]

"The Lowest Room" (1856), says Fass, "reveals a sharp awareness of sex roles as well as an ambivalence toward such roles." The "virtuous" sister is rewarded with a loving husband and a beautiful daughter, but the rebellious sister finally accepts her "role of the passively awaiting woman," spurning marriage, submitting to "an existence of self-conscious repression,"[115] and stoically awaiting her Savior: "I lift mine eyes up to the hills / From when my help shall come" (20).

In an essay on "Christina Rossetti: The Inward Pose," in *Shakesepare's Sisters: Feminist Essays on Women Poets* (1979), edited by Sandra M. Gilbert and Susan Gubar, Dolores Rosenblum, like Fass, sees Rossetti "compelled to adopt the persona of the lonely unsatisfied watcher, through endurance and humility conjuring up a wholly blameless apotheosis"—to be last, rather than first—but offers different reasons for its cause. Rosenblum feels that Rossetti "needed, for her psychic survival and her art, to hoard herself, perhaps because "the lonely watcher was a necessary condition for the writing of poetry" or "out of necessary conditions Rossetti invented the self that made poetry."[116]

In her later piece in *Victorian Poetry*, Rosenblum points out that Rossetti's poetry "is pervaded with references to masks, eyes, spectacles and displays, and to the acts of seeing, looking, staring, gazing and watching." Since she has alienated herself from a world that does not satisfy her, this "visual metaphor is central to her conception of self as woman and poet, woman and Christian. Rosenblum also contends that in her religious poems, Rossetti identifies herself with Christ because she, too, "experiences the isolation of self as spectacle, whether derided, or misunderstood, or merely appraised." Thus "Christ's isolation . . . becomes the adequate symbol for Rossetti's own predicament."[117]

Gilbert-Gubar in *The Madwoman in the Attic* agree with Rosenblum that Rossetti has been alienated from her world, but the alienation has been caused, they say, not by the poet's desire to be an onlooker because of her dissatisfaction with society, but because of societal constraints and the attitude that "female genius triggers uncontrollable sexual desires, and perhaps, conversely, uncontrollable sexual desires even cause the disease of female genius." This is implied in "Goblin Market" in the punishment—inner and outer disease—meted out to Jeanie and Laura for bartering with the goblin merchants for their luscious fruit (signifying sexuality). Thus some of the best female writers of the nineteenth century made whole poetic careers renouncing "the self-assertion lyric poetry traditionally demands" and demurely resigned themselves "to poetic isolation or obscurity." Christina Rossetti, Gilbert-Gubar assert, is a great nineteenth-century woman singer "of renunciation as necessity's highest and noblest virtue," building her poetry "on a willing acceptance of demure destitution, since "for the woman poet only renunciation, even anguish, can be a suitable source of song."[118] To them, Rossetti's "From House to Home" (1858) signifies "a paradise of self-gratifying art." In the poem, the poet-speaker tells of

> . . . a pleasure-place within my
>   soul,
> An earthly paradise supremely fair
>   that lured me from the goal. . . .
>
> [21]

Within this Eden, there is a castle of "white transparent glass, . . . songs and flowers and fruit" where

> . . . one like an angel walked with me
>   With spirit-discerning eyes like
>   flames of fire . . .
>   Fulfilling my desire:
>
> [21]

The angel, according to Gilbert-Gubar, symbolizes "a muse-like male spirit." But, because this inner paradise is a "pleasure-place," it soon turns into a place of exile for the poet-speaker, who, punitively forsaken by her muse, is condemned to bitter coldness, starvation, and old age. The tortured "Christ-like poet of Rossetti's vision drinks the bitterness of self-abnegation, and *then* sings," for "the woman artist can be strengthened 'to live' only through doses of paradoxically bitter-sweet pain":[119]

> Therefore in patience I possess my soul;
> Yea, therefore as a flint I set my
> face
> To pluck down, to build up again
> the whole—
> But in a distant place.

[25]

Cora Kaplan's essay comparing Christina Rossetti and Emily Dickinson finds that these two poets figure "much less prominently in the new feminist literary criticism than women novelists of the same period." They both concentrate on the inner life, in "virtual exclusion of the contemporary or social. . . . A conscious preoccupation with the constricting demands of feminity does not often surface in the poetry of either." Rossetti's and Dickinson's poems provide little grist for the mills of those who would assert that the twentieth century is a better world for women.

Rossetti *did* represent Victorian women's "internal struggles," Kaplan goes on to say, but, by "substituting fantasy for anger," was able to become prominent and participate in public discourse, a rare occurrence for women in Victorian England.[120] "Goblin Market" is actually "an exploration of women's sexual fantasy which includes suggestions of masochism, homoerotocism, rape, or incest." The images are unfinished and indistinct, either because of conscious or unconscious censorship, or out of sexual ignorance. Kaplan concludes that the poem "can be seen as a comical-tragical view of the erotic from the women's position with conscious and unconscious elements inextricably mingled."[121]

Gilbert-Gubar, while also detecting levels of meaning in "Goblin Market" particularly about and for women, are compelled to add that the poem "has recently begun to be something of a textual crux for feminist critics." In their view, "the indomitable Lizzie . . . may well seem almost a Victorian Amazon, a nineteenth-century reminder that 'sisterhood is powerful.'" There is a suggestion in this poem "that men *hurt* while women redeem," perhaps explaining why we are never told of Laura's and Lizzie's husbands and the fact that they eventually have daughters, not sons. It is as if

Rossetti is "dreamily positing an effectively matrilineal and matriarchal world, perhaps even, considering the strikingly sexual redemption scene between the sisters, a covertly (if ambivalently) lesbian world."[122]

Jerome J. McGann, writing in the Winter 1980 issue of *Victorian Studies*, states that "Goblin Market" stresses "independence from the erroneous belief that women need a man's love, otherwise they are incomplete." The poem, says he, illustrates love and marriage Victorian style. Although the sisters are finally married, they seem to have entered into "marriages of convenience." Their earlier sexual attraction to the goblins has turned to ashes "because it does not satisfy the women's fundamental desires." At the end of the poem, Laura and Lizzie are emotionally involved only with their children. When Laura relates to her children her earlier experiences with the goblins and how her sister bravely came to her rescue, it seems that feeling and sympathy are substituted for passion and eroticism; women and children are substituted for men. "Lizzie's heroic adventure on her sister's behalf dramatizes her integrity, her freedom from depending on the goblins."[123]

The Victorian marriage market disgusted Rossetti, McGann continues, and her heroines who choose lovers or marriage partners almost always meet with heartbreak. For example, in "A Triad" (1856), all three women—married and unmarried alike—fail because "each one's personality only exists in a dependency relation to something or someone else."[124] Thus personal independence, McGann claims, is one of Rossetti's main subjects.

Critics in all three eras discuss the way in which allegory, imagery, and symbolism provide a key to meaning and an element of style in Rossetti's poems, but critics of each period stress different aspects of figurative language. In the nineteenth century, it was allegory and imagery that engaged the critics; in the early part of the twentieth century, it was allegory, imagery, and symbolism in equal measure; and in the modern period, it is symbolism, with imagery a distant second and allegory hardly in the running. In earlier periods, many of Rossetti's critics emphasized figurative language in the religious and nature poems. Today's critics are less interested in the emblematic features of Rossetti's nature poems than in the figurative language expressing manifest or latent sexual passion and frustration they find in still other poems. "Goblin Market's" store of figurative language makes it common quarry for several of Rossetti's recent critics concerned with this aspect of her work.

The imagery in "Goblin Market" signals to Ellen Golub a conflict between regressive oral sadism and the reality-testing anal stage. The verse-image describing how Laura, as one Jeanie before her, "sucked and sucked the more / Fruits which that unknown orchard bore" suggests "the vision of a child at her mother's breast, and thus it incorporates the essential components of the oral stage." When the taster is forbidden to have another taste, she becomes frustrated "and gnashed her teeth for baulked desire, and wept / As if her heart would break"—in short, a rich example of a child "passing from oral passivity to oral sadism" as the mother weans her.[125]

Golub believes that Lizzie represents the alter ego of Laura, symbolic of the other half of the divided self. When Lizzie confronts the goblins, the imagery recalls "the next developmental stage: the anal." As indication of this, Golub offers the fact that the "soothing, plush and erotic imagery [of the fruits] yields to violence, action and dirt":

> Lashing their tails,
> They trod and hustled her,
> Elbowed and jostled her,
> Clawed with their nails,
> Barking, mewing, hissing, mocking,
> Tore her gown and soiled her stocking.
>
> [6]

Though the goblins cuffed and caught her,

> Lizzie uttered not a word;
> Would not open lip from lip
> Lest they should cram a mouthful in:
> But laughed in heart to feel the drip
> Of juice that syruped all her face.
>
> [7]

The imagery of this passage, Golub states, represents the power struggle between mother and child. Lizzie, "expressing the child's stubborn defiance of the withdrawal of love, . . . usurps the maternal hierarchy and sends the goblins into oblivion." As Lizzie passes on the fruit juices to Laura "the ego-split may be healed. . . . As Laura rapidly becomes Lizzie, the poem brings the fragments of self together in better harmony than they have ever been. . . . The fragments come together as Laura emerges from death to life."

Mrs. Frances and Miss Christina Rossetti, 1877.

Golub thus finds "Goblin Market" indicating "that a positive value may be attached to life and suffering, for the fall from innocence is, after all, an ascent into experience."[126]

Gisella Honnighausen writes in the Spring 1968 issue of *Victorian Poetry* that Rossetti's use of minute details suggests a deeper meaning: The imagery of the daisies planted on Jeanie's grave that do not flower—"I planted daisies there a year ago / That never blow"—are emblems of innocence in the language of flowers; they cannot sprout again on the grave of a sinner. The flowers, then, are not only a decorative detail, and not only a lovely depiction of nature, but emblems that serve a didactic purpose.[127]

A. A. De Vitis, in the Spring 1968 issue of *Journal of Popular Culture,* notes that the meaning of "Goblin Market" is made clearer by "an interpretation of the symbolism and an appreciation of imagery." He sees an equation drawn in the poem between day and night, . . . earth and water, fire and air." The goblins come "evening by evening" and set up their fruits along the grassy bank; yet the kernel stone that Laura brings home will not grow in her cottage garden, although she waters it with her tears. But once Laura is restored by the "fiery" antidote, her awareness of life in nature is keener than it has ever been. Thus, De Vitis believes, the world of day in the poem signifies the "world of practical reality"; the world of night signifies the "world of the imagination."[128]

John Adlard, writing for the general-interest magazine *The Contemporary Review* in September 1972, finds "a whole world of violence in the imagery" of "Goblin Market": a lily is borne down by a flood, flowers are beset by wasps, a town is besieged, an earthquake smashes a watchtower, lightning strikes a mast. To Rossetti, then, "the onset of sexual passion can shatter a life.[129]

Barbara Fass, in *Victorian Poetry,* states that in many of Rossetti's short verses, as well as in the longer poem "The Prince's Progress," an important image is the rosebud, "not of promised bliss, . . . but rather of frustration and failed hopes." In several poems, such as "An Apple Gathering" (1857), she notes, buds never flower, flowers fail to bear fruit; and in "Goblin Market" ripened fruit has a malignant effect.[130]

Modern critics see many more symbols in Rossetti's poetry than did Victorian reviewers and invest more meanings in symbols than did earlier twentieth-century critics. Lona Mosk Packer believes that the fruit sold by the goblin merchants in "Goblin Market" is the fruit that tempted Eve and, in Revelations 18:14, appears as "the fruit that thy soul lusteth after." She states that the theme of the poem is implicit: The joys of the earthly gratification of the senses is forbidden if one is to achieve spiritual redemption. "The lusciousness of the forbidden fruit and the charm of the little animal-faced goblins are but different aspects of nature, the core of which is sexual passion." The feast, Rossetti's familiar symbol of sexual love, Packer says, runs through the poem. Laura feasts lustfully on the fruit:

> Then sucked their fruit globes fair or red
> Sweeter than honey from the rock,
> Stronger than man-rejoicing wine,
> Clearer than water flowed that juice;
> She never tasted such before,
> How should it cloy with length of use?
> She sucked and sucked and sucked the more
> Fruits which the unknown orchard bore;
> She sucked until her lips were sore;
> Then flung the emptied rinds away.
>
> [2–3]

Packer believes the fruit represents physical consummation of love before marriage, a sin which Rossetti considers self-destructive. Lizzie

> . . . thought of Jeanie in her grave,
> Who should have been a bride;
> But who for joys brides hope to have
> Fell sick and died.
>
> [5]

To Packer the lines quoted above "represent two sorts of love, that which is domestic and legitimate, and the other, the outlawed love."[131]

Form is a major concern to both nineteenth- and twentieth-century critics of Rossetti's works but is examined to different purpose in each period. In the early period, critics sought the key to Rossetti's art of prosody in her use of metrics, diction, and rhythm. In the present period, critics seek additional insight into a poem's meaning in the same metrics, diction, rhythms, and in technique and structure as well. These same contemporary critics refer again and again to the companion pieces "Up-hill" (1858) and "Amor Mundi" (1865) in discussing Rossetti's uses of form to illuminate her ideas. The poems are a study in contrasts: "Up-hill" illustrates the difficulty of the returning ascent to Heaven and

"Amor Mundi" the ease of the descent to the path of folly, which leads to Hell.

Eugene J. Brzenk, for example, writing in the Winter 1972 issue of *Victorian Poetry*, points to the effective use of form in these two poems, which provide them with incremental meaning. The halting movements of the short lines made up largely of monosyllables produce the effect of the difficulty of reaching "that inn" in "Up-hill":

> Does the road wind up-hill all the way?
>   Yes, to the very end.
> Will the day's journey take the whole long day?
>   From morn to night, my friend.
>
> [339]

The tripping rhythm achieved by the poet's use of anapests and feminine and internal rhymes in "Amor Mundi," on the other hand, illustrates the ease with which the downhill path, "hell's own track," can be reached:

> 'Oh where are you going with your
>   love locks flowing,
> On the west wind blowing
>   along this valley track?'
> 'The downhill path is easy,
>   come with me and it please ye,
> We shall escape the uphill
>   by never turning back.'
>
> [374]

To Brzenk, the relationship of meter and rhythm to mood and theme is deliberate on the part of the poet. The changing, shifting meter of "Amor Mundi" actually characterizes the primrose-path mentality and is similar he finds, to Rossetti's nursery rhymes of *Sing-Song*. There is irony in the poem, he says, for the easy downhill path is ultimately revealed as hell and the laborious, uninviting ascent in "Up-hill" nevertheless promises that "Of labour you shall find the sum": "anyone familiar with Christina Rosetti's personal conception of salvation and the difficult road which leads to it recognizes that the whole movement is intended to convey this very austere conception."[132]

The diction in Rossetti's poems is of interest to more than half of her modern critics, for whom it is often a criterion for judgment of a work. Several refer specifically to the use of language in her religious poetry. For example, Nesca Robb states that Rossetti's words borrowed from the Scriptures "have sunk so deep into the writer's consciousness that they rise unbidden to her lips, faithful interpreters of her own thoughts, yet enriching her verse with memories and associations that no other words in the language possess."[133]

C. M. Bowra notes in *The Romantic Imagination* that Rossetti's "poetry of the soul's search for God and its struggles towards perfection is written in a language of remarkable simplicity." And the more serious she is, the less she decorates her verse, the fewer and more traditional her images, the more unpretentious her words, "But each word expresses exactly what she feels, and her sense of rhythm is so subtle that even in her darkest moments she can break into pure song." There are few versifiers, Bowra says, who can use homely, humble, commonplace words and phrases "only to rise to some sudden burst and thereby to show that even in the drabbest conditions there are possibilities of dazzling splendour."[134] Witness "What Would I Give" (1864), an example to Bowra of Rossetti's natural art of reflecting in simple language exactly what she feels—the yearning to cleanse some dark sin that has polluted her soul and has broken her heart:

> What would I give for a heart of flesh to
> warm me through,
> Instead of this heart of stone ice-cold
> whatever I do!
> Hard and cold and small, of all hearts
> the worst of all.
>   .   .   .   .
> What would I give for tears! not smiles
> but scalding tears
> To wash the black mark clean, and to thaw
> the frost of years,
> To wash the stain ingrain, and to make
> me clean again.

[363]

Bowra, referring again to "What Would I Give," notes that Rossetti has an unusual gift of varying the speed of a line by either punctuation or by stressing the important words:

The tremendous impact of this poem comes from many causes, but not least from the mastery of the metrical scheme. The internal rhythm in the third line of each stanza conveys with appalling force the chilling drop in the poet's spirit, the change from agonized dismay to something frozen and dark and insoluble. The rhythm responds with extraordinary sensitiveness to the movements of Christina's mood, and shows how at the centre of her anguish is a single gnawing grief.[135]

Structure is considered by contemporary critics another important factor in determining the meaning of Rossetti's poetry. For example, Theo Dombrowski, writing in the Spring 1976 issue of *Victorian Poetry* states that often the structure of Rossetti's poems reflects a "dualistic sensibility." The poet frequently uses the techniques of dialogue—statement and reply—to express a conflict of opposing viewpoints and antithesis—a rhetorical contrast of ideas—to establish a "dualistic framework." In many religious poems the antithesis is between time and eternity or earthly misery and heavenly bliss to express "the torment of a trapped soul longing for escape." In several secular poems, the antithesis is between life and death, joy and sorrow, present and past (or future), or hope and despair. Repeatedly, Rossetti depends upon antithetical elements, says Dombrowski, "to bring a theme into focus to underline the dual nature of an experience," or to develop a two-part contrast, as in "She Sat and Sang Alway" (1848):[136]

> She sat and sang alway
>   By the green margin of a stream,
> Watching the fishes leap and play
>   Beneath the glad sunbeam.
>
> I sat and wept alway
>   Beneath the moon's most shadowy
>   beam,
> Watching the blossoms of the May
>   Weep leaves into the stream.
>
> I wept for memory;
>   She sang for hope that is so fair:
> My tears were swallowed by the sea;
>   Her songs died on the air.

[290]

In the December 1973 issue of *Victorian Poetry*, K. E. Janowitz asserts that the poem "Spring" (1859), "with its irregular stanzas and irregular rhyme scheme and line length is a superb example of Christina's skill in experimenting with form." The second line of the poem—"Seeds, and roots, and stones of fruit"—he says, is an example of strong Trochaic rhythm which "conveys a sense that all growing things are now again in motion and ready to emerge from beneath the earth." In lines 10 through 12 of the poem, in order to invoke the rejuvenating forces of nature that create new life, the poet begins each line with its verb rather than its noun:

> Blows the thaw-wind pleasantly
> Drips the soaking rain,
> By fits looks down the waking sun.

Janowitz notes that the pair of couplets that conclude stanza 2 accelerate the pace of the poem:

> Curled-headed ferns sprout in the lane;
> Birds sing and pair again.

The rise in tempo that continues in the third stanza is effected by the use of a melodious iambic couplet (actually the first two lines of a triplet):

> There is no time like Spring,
> When life's alive in everything.

But the second trimeter in the last stanza of the poem completes the thought that the miraculous rebirth of nature is only transitory;[137]

> There is no time like Spring that passes by,
> Now newly born, and now
> Hastening to die.
>
> [345–46]

For Marya Zaturenska, "Amor Mundi" takes it place as Rossetti's greatest work because "of the technical skill of the poem" and the appeal to the ear in which "we hear the sound of human voices in warning, in anger, and in despair." She hears in the terror and anger voiced in this poem "Christina carrying on a dialogue between her own passionate sensuous nature, and that strong and self-imposed austerity which was never quite to overcome it."[138]

Georgina Battiscombe examines in *Christina Rossetti* (1965) the poet's use of the Rondeau technique—the sixteenth-century poetic style that enjoyed a limited return to fashion at the end of the Victorian Age and featured a repetition of phrases to gain unusual effect. "Sleeping At Last" (circa 1893) is such a poem. It voices the poet's yearning for the sleep of death that obliterates the travails of life:

> Sleeping at last, the trouble and
> tumult over,
> Sleeping at last, the struggle and
> horror past,
> Cold and white, out of sight of friend
> and of lover,
> Sleeping at last.
>
> No more a tired heart downcast
> or overcast,
> No more pangs that wring or shifting
> fears that hover,
> Sleeping at last in a dreamless
> sleep locked fast.
>
> Fast asleep. Singing birds in their
> leafy cover
> Cannot wake her, nor shake her
> the gusty blast.
> Under the purple thyme and the
> purple clover
> Sleeping at last.
>
> [417]

Rossetti's poetry "was a poetry of concentration rather than development," Battiscombe says, "and therefore particularly adapted to this form with its repetition both of phrase and rhyme, the metre as it were folding inwards upon the central idea of the poem."[139]

A single critic in the modern period addresses what he calls Rossetti's smallness of range and paucity of ideas. Stuart Curran, in his 1971 *Victorian Poetry* article, concludes that "she has only one real subject, mortality, and the variety of her treatment is never extensive." Furthermore, "her stock of images is small, and they are seldom developed in striking or suggestive ways"; and because of her "temperamental austerity" her range is small. He admits that Rossetti wrote with ease—"her single most prominent poetic attribute"—but he claims that she lacked a sense of direction and "has so little to say that she can seldom venture beyond a small effort." Though possessed of considerable technical skill, "she lacked the mental prowess to develop it." She is not concerned with the state of man or with the state of the church, only herself. She is humble, submissive, and unpretentious, yet

> a great poet cannot be unpretentious: he dares and questions; he attempts to answer. . . . Her poetry is largely devoid of sharp observation, whether intellectual or imaginative. . . . but she has the not inconsiderable gift of felicitous music. She falls back on pretty language, the bane of so many women poets.[140]

Curran considers that Rossetti showed no growth during her poetic career. At best her lines are "shallow, melodious, totally at ease with themselves, and, as ever, unpretentious"—here Curran, like Battiscombe, cites "Sleeping At Last" (circa 1893). However, in spite of her limitations—"lack of depth of image" and "of complicated thought"—Curran concludes that Rossetti is essentially a "spontaneous poet" who "never labors the magic out of her lyrics."[141]

F. L. Lucas acknowledges that Rossetti knew very little about books and about life itself, but however few the things she knew, "she knew them well; and one of them was her own mind."[142]

For Lionel Stevenson, author of *The Pre-Raphaelite Poets* (1972), Rossetti's contribution to English poetry itself is quite extensive: "Her range encompasses romantic narrative, symbolic dream-visions, realistic dramatic monologues, imitation folk-ballads, playful fantasies, a cantata [All Thy Works Praise Thee, O Lord"], a pageant ["The Months"], as well as hundreds of lyrics and sonnets."[143]

The 1940–82 period has seen heightened interest in the United States in Christina Rossetti's works, most notably by critics who fall under the rubric "feminist." Familiarity with Freudian and Jungian concepts of the unconscious and with various forms of sexuality that were rarely even acknowledged publicly in earlier eras have been influences in their approach to Rossetti's poems. Thus we are given evidence of the poet's expressions of childhood eroticism and sexual fantasies; of libidinous desires that erupted despite all attempts at repressing them; of the endeavor to use poetry to dramatize restrictions on Victorian women or to mythologize her own barren life; of life choices that were the means for attaining artistic freedom.

In these efforts, "Goblin Market" has served as a prime source. One hopes that similar attention will be paid to still other works, illuminating and enlarging their meaning in turn. One hopes too that the common ground between Christina Rossetti and other poets of her era, both male and female, will be explored as earnestly.

The present period has also seen a new, and welcome, concentration by reviewers on a small number of poems, in contrast to earlier attempts to survey the entire spectrum of the poet's works. With the tools of the modern critic in hand—the new "psychological systems" that Daiches has described—they have been able to provide greater insight into individual Rossetti works, most notably in examining the symbolism in that richest of all symbolic works, "Goblin Market," and in a number of poems overlooked or given short shrift in early periods, such as "The Lowest Room" "A Nightmare," "My Dream," and "A Sketch."

One appreciates, for example, the efforts of C. M. Bowra, who, in examining "Echo," "Twice," and "What Would I Give," illuminates the conflicts in Rossetti's life without losing sight of the poet's own "passionate convictions" as given voice in her poetry. In some other hands the efforts to unearth new meanings in the poetry allow the critic to become a candidate for the Sontag "excavation" award. Ellen Golub, for one, places "Goblin Market" and its author on a couch and, using clinical procedures and a basic Freudian text, pushes the analysis to absurd limits; she manages to obscure the very poems she is trying to explain.

Similarly, biographer Lona Mosk Packer, having "found" Scott, assumes that the Rossetti-Scott relationship is lurking behind every passionate word the poet writes, that he inhabits every buzzard she describes. Assumption becomes fact, and no doubts may intrude upon the truth of what comes after. She admits of no other valid interpretations.

The first substantial attempts at a systematic approach to Rossetti's poetry are seen in the mythic criticism provided by Winston Weathers in his explanation of "Goblin Market," "A Triad," and "Maiden-Song"; and by Nesca A. Robb in "Eve," "Dream-Love," and "Long Barren." Still, critics are just beginning to employ Jungian postulates to interpret Rossetti's poems, and doubtless these will be brought to bear in much new criticism in the future.

One thing is clear: critics—whether Freudian, Jungian, feminist, or of a tradition yet to be named—will continue to search the poetic works of Christina Rossetti for the riches still to be mined.

Notes

Introduction

1. The present work incorporates some of the material that appeared in "A Comparative Study of Nineteenth and Twentieth Century Criticism of Selected Poems of Christina Rossetti," the author's doctoral dissertation presented at New York University in 1978. That material—as well as the scope and aim of the initial undertaking—has undergone considerable revision and expansion.

2. Volume 1 of *Christina Georgina Rossetti, 1830–1894. The Complete Poems of Christina Rossetti*, Variorium Edition, was published by Louisiana State University Press in 1979. Two more volumes, with textual notes, edited by R. W. Crump are projected. When completed, volumes 1 and 2 will contain the collections that were individually published, along with the poems added to each collection in subsequent editions. The third volume will contain poems printed but uncollected and poems seen only in manuscript. According to Sandra M. Gilbert and Susan Gubar, in *Shakespeare's Sisters* (1979), Hans B. de Groot of the University of Toronto is also planning an edition of Christina Rossetti's poetry (p. 312). Two bibliographical guides to Rossetti's works and those of her critics may be useful to readers of the present study. Rebecca S. Weideman's "A Critical Bibliography of Christina Rossetti" (Ph.D. diss., University of Texas at Austin, 1979) contains three annotated sections: bibliographic aids, writings of Christina Rossetti with reviews, and biography and criticism, arranged in chronological order from 1862 to 1969. R. W. Crump's *Christina Rossetti: A Reference Guide* (Boston: G. K. Hall & Co., 1976), which he calls "a revised and reorganized version" (p. 136) of Weideman's earlier dissertation, contains brief annotations of writings about Christina Rossetti from 1862 to 1973, arranged in chronological order. Crump here points out the need for "a comprehensive examination on the valuation of Christina's literary accomplishments" (p. ix).

3. Elisabeth Luther Cary, *The Rossettis: Dante Gabriel and Christina* (New York: C. P. Putnam's Sons, 1900), pp. 262–65.

4. Mackenzie Bell, *Christina Rossetti: A Biographical and Critical Study*, 4th ed. (London: Thomas Burleigh, 1898), p. 319.

5. William Michael Rossetti, *Some Reminiscences* (London: Brown Langham, 1906) 1:65.

6. Christina Georgina Rossetti, *The Poetical Works of Christina Georgina Rossetti. With Memoir and Notes by William Michael Rossetti* (London: Macmillan, 1906), p. lii.

7. William E. Fredeman, review of *Christina Rossetti*, by Lona Mosk Packer, *Victorian Studies* 8 (September 1964): 72.

Chapter 1. The Poet-Saint

1. "Christina Rossetti's Poems," *Catholic World* (24 October 1876): 126–27.

2. Christina Georgina Rossetti, *The Poetical Works of Christina Georgina Rossetti. With Memoir and Notes by William Michael Rossetti* (London: Macmillan, 1906), pp. 146–47, hereafter referred to as *The Poetical Works*. All lines from Christina Rossetti's poetry quoted in this study are taken from this volume, and page numbers are cited in brackets throughout the text.

3. "Christina Rossetti's Poems," *Catholic World* 24 (October 1876): 127.

4. "Christina Georgina Rossetti," *Dial*, 16 January 1895, pp. 37–39.

5. Edmund K. Chambers, "Review of Miss Rossetti's Verse," *Academy* 45 (February 1894): 164.

6. [Arthur Symons], "Miss Rossetti's Poetry," *London Quarterly Review* 68 (July 1887): 344.

7. Ibid., p. 342.

8. "Christina Rossetti," *Saturday Review*, 5 January 1895, p. 6.

9. Lily Watson, "Christina Rossetti," *Sunday at Home*, 5 May 1894, p. 428.

10. "Miss Rossetti's Poems," *Saturday Review*, February 1896, p. 196.

11. A. Smellie, "Christina Rossetti and Her Message," *Wesleyan Methodist Magazine* 118 (1895): 204–5.

12. Lionel Johnson, "Literature: Miss Rossetti and Mrs. Alexander," *Academy*, 25 July 1896, p. 59.

13. "Christina Rossetti," *Saturday Review*, 5 January 1895, p. 6.

14. "Poems by Mr. and Miss Rossetti," *Ecclesiastic and Theologian* 24 (September 1962): 427.

15. [Symons], "Miss Rossetti's Poetry," pp. 344–45.

16. Alice Meynell, "Christina Rossetti," *New Review* 12 (February 1895): 203.

17. "Christina Rossetti's Poems," *Catholic World* 24 (October 1876): 125.

18. Mackenzie Bell, *Christina Rossetti: A Biographical and Critical Study*, 4th ed. (London: Thomas Burleigh, 1898), p. 206.

19. "Contemporary Poets and Versifiers," *Edinburgh Review* 178 (October 1892): 495.

20. "Poems by Mr. and Miss Rossetti," *Ecclesiastic and Theologian* 24 (September 1962): 427–29.

21. [F. A. Rudd], "Christina Rossetti," *Catholic World* 4 (March 1867): 839.

22. R. R. Bowker, "London as a Literary Center," *Harper Magazine* 76 (May 1888): 827.

23. [Symons], "Miss Rossetti's Poetry," pp. 339–40.

24. James Benjamin Kenyon, "Dante Gabriel Rossetti and His Sister Christina," *Methodist Review* 78 (September 1896): 751.

25. Christabel R. Coleridge, "The Poetry of Christina Rossetti," *Monthly Packet* 89 (March 1895): 280.

26. Mrs. Charles Eliot Norton, " 'The Angel in the House' and 'The Goblin Market,' " *Macmillan's Magazine*, 7 September 1863, p. 404.

27. Sir Edmond Goose, "Christina Rossetti," *Century Magazine* 46 (June 1893): 215.

28. [Symons], "Miss Rossetti's Poetry," p. 340.

29. Alice Law, "The Poetry of Christina G. Rossetti," *Westminster Review* 143 (April 1895): 447.

30. [Symons], "Miss Rossetti's Poetry," p. 341.

31. "Christina Rossetti's Poems," *Catholic World* 24 (October 1876): 124.

32. [Symons], "Miss Rossetti's Poetry," p. 341.

33. "Christina Rossetti," *Saturday Review*, 5 January 1895, pp. 5–6.
34. Bell, *Christina Rossetti*, pp. 216–17.
35. Harry Baxton Foreman, "Criticism on Contemporaries. No. VI. The Rossettis. Part 1. Christina Rossetti," *Tinsley's Magazine* 5 (August 1869): 63–64.
36. Arthur Christopher Benson, "Christina Rossetti," *National Review* 26 (February 1895): 757.
37. Gosse, "Christina Rossetti," pp. 216–17.
38. Benson, "Christina Rossetti," p. 757.
39. [Symons], "Miss Rossetti's Poetry," p. 347.
40. Law, "The Poetry of Christina Rossetti," p. 451.
41. "Miss Rossetti's New Poems," *Athenaeum*, 10 September 1881, p. 328.
42. "The Rossettis," *Literary World*, 5 November 1881, p. 396.
43. T. Hall Caine, *Academy*, 27 August 1881, p. 152.
44. Benson, "Christina Rossetti," p. 758.
45. "Miss Rossetti's Poems," *Saturday Review*, February 1896, p. 196.
46. Gosse, "Christina Rossetti," p. 217.
47. Chambers, "Miss Rossetti's Verse," p. 163.
48. [Symons], "Miss Rossetti's Poetry," p. 342.
49. Bayard Taylor, "Christina Rossetti," *Critical Essays and Literary Notes* (New York: G. P. Putnam's Sons, 1880), pp. 330–32.
50. [Symons], "Miss Rossetti's Poetry," p. 340.
51. Law, "Poetry of Christina Rossetti," p. 447.
52. Benson, "Christina Rossetti," p. 757.
53. Richard Le Gallienne, "Christina Rossetti," *Academy*, 7 February 1891, p. 131.
54. Law, "The Poetry of Christina Rossetti," p. 447.
55. "Christina Rossetti's Poems," *Catholic World* 24 (October 1876): 122.
56. Foreman, "Criticism," pp. 60–62.
57. Ibid., pp. 62–65.
58. Ibid.
59. Ibid.
60. Law, "The Poetry of Christina Rossetti," pp. 445–46.
61. Coleridge, "Poetry of Christina Rossetti," p. 278.
62. Bell, *Christina Rossetti*, pp. 262–63.
63. [Symons], "Miss Rossetti's Poetry," p. 347.
64. William Michael Rossetti, "Memoir" in Christina Georgina Rossetti, *The Poetical Works*, pp. 1ii–1iii.
65. Benson, "Christina Rossetti," p. 756.
66. Ibid., pp. 757–58.
67. Law, "The Poetry of Christina Rossetti," pp. 449–50.
68. [Symons], "Miss Rossetti's Poetry," p. 344.
69. *London Quarterly Review* 87 (October 1896): 11–13.
70. *Edinburgh Review* 188 (April 1896): 514.
71. W. M. Payne, *Dial*, 6 April 1896, p. 205.
72. Benson, "Christina Rossetti," pp. 756–78.
73. Ibid., p. 756.
74. Smellie, "Christina Rossetti's Message," p. 205.
75. "Miss Rossetti's New Poems," *Athenaeum*, 10 September 1881, pp. 327–28.
76. *Athenaeum*, 23 June 1866, pp. 824–25.
77. [Symons], "Miss Rossetti's Poetry," pp. 345–46.
78. Benson, "Christina Rossetti," p. 753.

79. Bell, *Christina Rossetti*, p. 222.
80. [Symons], "Miss Rossetti's Poetry," p. 347.
81. Law, "Poetry of Christina Rossetti," pp. 444–45.
82. "Christina Rossetti," *Saturday Review*, 5 January 1895, p. 6.
83. Ibid., pp. 5–6.
84. Benson, "Christina Rossetti," pp. 754–55.
85. "Miss Rossetti's Poems," *Saturday Review*, February 1896, p. 196.
86. [Symons], "Miss Rossetti's Poetry," pp. 338–39.
87. Ibid., p. 339.
88. Le Gallienne, "Christina Rossetti," p. 120.
89. *Literary World* (Boston) 6 (May 1876): 181–82.
90. [Symons], "Miss Rossetti's Poetry," p. 338.
91. Meynell, "Christina Rossetti," p. 204.
92. Chambers, "Miss Rossetti's Verse," p. 163.
93. [Symons], "Miss Rossetti's Poetry," p. 345.
94. Benson, "Christina Rossetti," pp. 760–61.
95. [Symons], "Miss Rossetti's Poetry," p. 345.
96. Johnson, "Literature," p. 59.
97. *Literature*, 22 January 1898 pp. 66–68.
98. "Christina Rossetti's Poems," *Catholic World* 24 (October 1876): 129.
99. Ibid.
100. Gosse, "Christina Rossetti," p. 215.
101. Kenyon, "His Sister Christina," p. 751.
102. "Christina G. Rossetti," *Catholic World* 4 (March 1867): 845–46.
103. Gosse, "Christina Rossetti," pp. 213–15.
104. Law, "Poetry of Christina Rossetti," p. 448.
105. Kenyon, "His Sister Christina," p. 750.
106. Law, "Poetry of Christina Rossetti," p. 448.
107. "Christina Rossetti's Poems," *Catholic World* 24 (October 1876): 124–25.
108. Amy Levy, "The Poetry of Christina Rossetti," *Woman's World* (London) 1 (February 1888): 180.
109. "Some Women Poets," *Living Age*, 1 April 1899, pp. 26–34.
110. "Christina Rossetti," *Saturday Review*, 5 January 1895, p. 5.
111. "Miss Rossetti's Poems," *Saturday Review*, February 1896, p. 196.
112. "Christina Rossetti's Poems," *Catholic World* 24 (October 1876): 126–27.
113. Theodore Watts-Dunton, "Christina Georgina Rossetti," *Athenaeum*, (15 January 1896), p. 208.
114. Smellie, "Christina Rossetti's Message," pp. 204–5.
115. "Christina Rossetti," *Saturday Review*, 5 January 1895, p. 6.
116. [W. Robertson Nicoll], "Mr. Bell's 'Christina Rossetti,'" *Bookman* 13 (February 1898): 154.
117. "Miss Rossetti's Poems," *Saturday Review*, February 1896, p. 196.

Chapter 2. The Woman as Poet

1. A. J. Green-Armytage, *Maids of Honour* (London: Blackwood, 1906), pp. 286–87.
2. Edith Birkhead, *Christina Rossetti and Her Poetry* (London: George G. Harrap & Co., 1930), pp. 36–37.

3. Virginia Moore, "Letters and Comments: Christina Rossetti's Centennial," *Yale Review* 20 (December 1930): 429.

4. Frances Winmar [pseudonym, Frances Grebanier), *Poor Splendid Wings: The Rosettis and Their Circle* (Boston: Little, Brown, 1933), p. 27.

5. Winwar, *Poor Splendid Wings,* p. 30.

6. Violet Hunt, *The Wife of Rossetti* (New York: E. P. Dutton, 1932), p. xiii.

7. Eudora Zaidee Green, "Saint by Chance," *English Review* 62 (March 1936): 332–37.

8. Eleanor Walter Thomas, *Christina Georgina Rossetti* (1931; reprint ed., New York: AMS Press, 1966), p. 197.

9. Christina Georgina Rossetti, *The Poetical Works of Christina Georgina Rossetti, With Memoir and Notes by William Michael Rossetti* (London: Macmillan, 1906), pp. 241–42, hereafter referred to as *The Poetical Works.* All lines from Christina Rossetti's poetry quoted in this study are taken from this volume and page numbers are cited in brackets throughout the text.

10. Percy H. Osmond, *The Mystical Poets of the English Church* (London: Society for the Promotion of Christian Knowledge, 1919), p. 410.

11. Eugene Mason, *A Book of Preferences in Literature* (New York: E. P. Dutton, 1915), pp. 118–21.

12. Moore, "Letters and Comments," p. 429.

13. Sister M. Madeleva, *Chaucer's Nuns and Other Essays* (Port Washington, N.Y.: Kennikat Press, 1925), pp. 123–26.

14. Osbert Burdett, *The Beardsley Period* (London: John Lany The Bodley Heat Ltd., 1925), p. 131.

15. Virginia Woolf, *The Second Common Reader* (New York: Harcourt, Brace & Company, 1932), p. 264.

16. Thomas, *Christina Georgina Rossetti,* p. 162.

17. Fredegond Shove, *Christina Rossetti: A Study* (1931; reprint ed. New York: Octagon Press, 1969), pp. 78–79.

18. Joseph L. Reilly, "Christina Rossetti," *America: A Catholic Review of the Week,* 14 February 1931, p. 460.

19. Joseph L. Reilly, *Dear Prue's Husband and Other People* (New York: Macmillan, 1932), p. 146.

20. Geoffrey W. Rossetti, "Christina Rossetti," *Criterion* 10 (October 1930): 104.

21. Mary Frances Sandars, *The Life of Christina Rossetti* (London: Hutchinson Co. [Publishers] Limited, 1930), pp. 120–21.

22. Frank Jewett Mather, Jr., "The Rossettis," *Bookman* (New York) 49 (April 1919): 142.

23. Shove, *Christina Rossetti,* p. xi.

24. Ibid., p. 84.

25. Anne Kimball Tuell, "Christina Rossetti," in *A Victorian at Bay* (Boston: Marshall, Jones, 1932), p. 51.

26. Ford Madox Hueffer, "Christina Rossetti and Pre-Raphaelite Love," in *Memories and Impressions: A Study in Atmospheres* (New York: Harper, 1911), pp. 67–68.

27. Margaret Mackenzie, "Fettered Christina Rossetti," *Thought: Fordham University Quarterly* 7 (January 1932): 42.

28. Dorothy Margaret Stuart, *Christina Rossetti* (London: Macmillan, 1930), pp. 176–82.

29. Thomas, *Christina Georgina Rossetti,* p. 158.

30. Ibid., p. 142.

31. Louis Cazamian, *A History of English Literature: Modern Times* (1927; rev. ed., London: J. M. Dent & Sons, Ltd., 1930), pp. 1180–81.

32. Mason, *Book of Preferences*, p. 122.

33. Thomas, *Christina Georgina Rossetti*, p. 156.

34. Oliver Elton, *A Survey of English Literature, 1830–1880*, 2 vols. (1920; reprint ed., London: Edward Arnold, Ltd., 1955), 2:23–24.

35. Mather, "The Rossettis," p. 142.

36. Stuart, *Christina Rossetti*, p. 77.

37. Geoffrey W. Rosetti, "Christina Rossetti," p. 104.

38. Birkhead, *Christina Rossetti*, p. 139.

39. Ibid., p. 61.

40. Thomas, *Christina Georgina Rossetti*, p. 139.

41. Ibid., pp. 140–41.

42. George Lowther, "Christina Rossetti," *Contemporary Review* 104 (November 1913): 683.

43. Thomas, *Christina Georgina Rossetti*, p. 142.

44. Reilly, *Dear Prue's Husband and Other People*, p. 161.

45. Claude C. H. Williamson, "A Few Lines on Christina Rossetti," *Writers of Three Centuries, 1789–1914* (Philadelphia: George W. Jacobs & Co., 1915), p. 271.

46. Desmond Lionel Morse-Boycott, "Christina Rossetti: 1830–1894," *Lead, Kindly Light: Studies of the Saints and Heroes of the Oxford Movement* (New York: Macmillan, 1933), p. 127.

47. Anna Bunston de Bary, "The Poetry of Christina," *Poetry Review* (London) 1 (May 1912): 208.

48. Thomas, *Christina Georgina Rossetti*, pp. 182–83.

49. Ford Madox Hueffer, "The Collected Poems of Christina Rossetti," *Fortnightly Review* 75 (March 1904): 402–3.

50. Thomas, *Christina Georgina Rossetti*, p. 142.

51. Green-Armytage, *Maids of Honour*, pp. 294–95.

52. Arthur Clutton-Brock, *More Essays on Religion* (London: Methuen, 1927; reprint ed., Freeport, N.Y.: Books for Libraries Press, 1971), pp. 20–21.

53. George Saintsbury, *Historical Manuel of English Prosody from the Twelfth Century to the Present Day* (London: Macmillan, 1910), 3:353–59.

54. Cazamian, *History of English Literature*, p. 1181.

55. Geoffrey W. Rossetti, "Christina Rossetti," pp. 102–3.

56. Hueffer, "The Collected Poems of Christina Rossetti," pp. 397–98.

57. Geoffrey W. Rossetti, "Christina Rossetti," pp. 106–8.

58. Elisabeth Luther Cary, *The Rossettis: Dante Gabriel and Christina* (New York: G. P. Putnam's Sons, 1900), pp. 262–64.

59. Muriel Kent, "Christina Rossetti: A Reconsideration," *Contemporary Review* 37 (January 1931): 213–16.

60. Morton Dauwen Zabel, "Christina Rossetti and Emily Dickinson," *Poetry* 37 (January 1931): 213–16.

61. Kathleen C. Green, "Christina Rossetti: A Study and Some Comparisons," *Cornhill Magazine* 69 (December 1930): 665.

62. Moore, "Letters and Comments," p. 424.

63. William Henry Hudson, *A Short History of English Literature in the Nineteenth Century* (London: G. Bell & Sons, 1918), p. 145.

64. Amelia Marjorie Bald, "Christina Rossetti: 1839–1894," *Women-Writers of the Nineteenth Century* (New York: Russell & Russell, 1963).

65. Alexander Hamilton Thompson, "Christina Rossetti," *Cambridge History of English* Literature (New York: Macmillan, 1917), vol. 13, part 2, pp. 153–56.

66. Lafcadio Hearn, "Miss Rossetti," *Complete Lectures: A History of English Literature* (One-volume ed., Tokyo: Hokuseido, 1934), pp. 749–51.

67. John Cunliffe, *Leaders of the Victorian Revolution* (New York: D. Appleton-Century Co., 1934), p. 239.

68. Sir Edward Boyle, *Biographical Essays, 1790–1890* (London: Oxford University Press, 1936; reprint ed., Freeport, N.Y.: Books for Libraries Press, 1968), pp. 202–3.

69. Mather, "The Rossettis," p. 143.

70. Arthur Waugh, *Reticence in Literature* (London: J. G. Wilson, 1915), pp. 150–52.

71. Edward Thomas, *The Last Sheaf: Essays* (Frome, Great Britain: Butler & Tanner, Ltd., 1928), pp. 65–70.

72. Paul Elmer More, "Christina Rossetti," *Atlantic Monthly* 94 (December 1904): 818–19.

73. Ibid., p. 816.

74. Lowther, "Christina Rossetti," p. 687.

75. Cary, *The Rossettis,* p. 251.

76. Green-Armytage, *Maids of Honour,* pp. 295–96.

77. Hueffer, "Christina Rossetti and Pre-Raphaelite Love," p. 61.

78. "Victorian Romantics," *Times Literary Supplement,* 14 November 1929, p. 919.

79. Hugh Walker and Mrs. Hugh Walker, *Outlines of Victorian Literature* (Cambridge, England: University Press, 1919), pp. 82–83.

80. Green-Armytage, *Maids of Honour,* p. 297.

81. Shove, *Christina Rossetti,* p. 60.

82. Thomas, *Christina Georgina Rossetti,* p. 181.

83. Ibid., p. 149.

84. Ibid., pp. 128–29.

85. Shove, *Christina Rossetti,* p. 84.

86. Elton, *Survey of English Literature,* 2:28–29.

87. Sir Walter Raleigh, *Letters of Sir Walter Raleigh,* ed. Lady Raleigh (London: Methuen & Co., 1926), 1:164.

88. Madeleva, *Chaucer's Nuns,* pp. 124–25.

Chapter 3. The Poet Psychoanalyzed

1. Margaret Sawtell, *Christina Rossetti: Her Life and Religion* (London: A. R. Mobray & Co., 1955), p. 84.

2. Christina Georgina Rossetti, *The Poetical Works of Christina Georgina Rossetti. With Memoir and Notes by William Michael Rossetti* (London: Macmillan, 1906), pp. 60–61, hereafter referred to as *The Poetical Works.* All lines from Christina Rossetti's poetry quoted in this study are taken from this volume, and page numbers are cited in brackets throughout the text.

3. Sawtell, *Her Life and Religion,* p. 85.

4. F. L. Lucas, "Christina Rossetti," *Ten Victorian Poets,* 3d ed. (Cambridge, England: University Press, 1940), p. 130.

5. David Daiches, *Critical Approaches to Literature* (Englewood Cliffs, N.J.: Prentice-Hall, 1956), p. 345.

6. Susan Sontag, *Against Interpretation and Other Essays* (New York: Farrar, Straus, & Giroux, 1966), p. 6.

7. Stuart Curran, "The Lyric Voice of Christina Rossetti," *Victorian Poetry* 9, no. 3 (Autumn 1971): 290.

8. Lucas, "Christina Rossetti" pp. 123–24.

9. C. M. Bowra, *The Romantic Imagination* (New York: Oxford University Press, 1961), p. 261.

10. Marya Zaturenska, *Christina Rossetti: A Portrait with Background* (New York: Macmillan, 1949), p. 159.

11. Georgina Battiscombe, *Christina Rossetti: A Divided Life* (New York: Holt, Rinehart & Winston, 1981), p. 116, hereafter referred to as *A Divided Life.*

12. Ibid., pp. 94–95.

13. Zaturenska, *A Portrait with Background*, pp. 150–51.

14. Georgina Battiscombe, *Christina Rossetti* (London: Longmans, Green & Co., 1965), p. 21, hereafter referred to as *Christina Rossetti.*

15. Lona Mosk Packer, *Christina Rossetti* (Berkeley: University of California Press, 1963), pp. 52–53.

16. Ibid., pp. 186–87.

17. William E. Fredeman, *Victorian Studies* 8 (September 1964): 72–76.

18. Nesca A. Robb, "Christina Rossetti," *Four in Exile* (London: Hutchinson & Co., 1948), p. 103.

19. Jerome J. McGann, "Christina Rossetti's Poems: A New Edition and a Revaluation," *Victorian Studies* 23 (Winter 1980): 246–47.

20. Bowra, *Romantic Imagination*, p. 262.

21. Packer, *Christina Rossetti*, p. 112.

22. Ibid., p. 112.

23. Battiscombe, *Christina Rossetti*, p. 21.

24. Battiscombe, *A Divided Life*, p. 112.

25. Bowra, *Romantic Imagination*, p. 254–55.

26. Geoffrey Grigson, "Between Flesh and Spirit," *Times Literary Supplement,* 11 April 1980, p. 409.

27. Germaine Greer, "Introduction," in *Goblin Market* by Christina Rossetti (New York: Stonehill Publishing Co., 1975), p. xvi.

28. Thomas Barnett Swann, *Wonder and Whimsy* (Francetown, N.H.: Marshall Jones Co., 1960), pp. 50–51.

29. Daiches, *Critical Approaches*, p. 340.

30. Packer, *Christina Rossette*, pp. 94–95.

31. Battiscombe, *A Divided Life*, p. 109.

32. Packer, *Christina Rossetti*, p. 267.

33. Lionel Trilling, *The Liberal Imagination: Essays on Literature and Society* (Garden City, N.Y.: Anchor Books, 1953), p. 32.

34. Ralph A. Bellas, *Christina Rossetti* (Boston: Twayne Publishers, 1977), p. 62.

35. William Michael Rossetti, "Notes," *The Poetical Works*, p. 480.

36. Packer, *Christina Rossetti*, pp. 112–13.

37. Cora Kaplan, "The Indefinite Disclosed: Christina Rossetti and Emily Dickinson," in *Women Writing and Writing about Women*, ed. Mary Jacobus (New York: Barnes & Noble Books, 1979), pp. 70–73.

38. Robb, *Four in Exile*, p. 118.

39. Zaturenska, *A Portrait with Background* pp. 54–57.

40. Diane D'Amico, "Christina Rossetti's *Later Life:* The Neglected Sonnet Sequence," *Victorian Institute Journal* 9 (1980–81): 26.

41. Battiscombe, *A Divided Life*, pp. 78–79.

42. Dolores Rosenblum, "Christina Rossetti's Religious Poetry: Watching, Looking, Keeping Vigil," *Victorian Poetry*, 20, no. 1 (Spring 1982): 46–47.

43. Bowra, *Romantic Imagination*, p. 256.

44. Packer, *Christina Rossetti*, p. 123.

45. Ibid., pp. 195–96.

46. Robb, *Four in Exile*, p. 113.

47. Bowra, *Romantic Imagination*, pp. 251–52.

48. Daiches, *Critical Approaches*, p. 345.

49. Lucas, "Christina Rossetti," pp. 120–36.

50. K. E. Janowitz, "The Antipodes of Self: Three Poems by Christina Rossetti," *Victorian Poetry* 11, no. 3 (14 December 1973): 198–204.

51. Packer, *Christina Rossetti*, pp. 56–66.

52. Swann, *Wonder and Whimsy*, pp. 71–72.

53. Conrad Daniel Festa, "Studies in Christina Rossetti's 'Goblin Market' and Other Poems" (Ph.D. diss., University of South Carolina, 1969), p. 37.

54. Martine Watson Brownley, "Love and Sensuality in Christina Rossetti's 'Goblin Market,'" *Essays in Literature* 6, no. 1 (Spring 1979): 184.

55. Ellen Moers, *Literary Women* (Garden City, N.Y.: Doubleday & Co. 1976), p. 104.

56. Ibid., pp. 105–6.

57. Ibid., pp. 102–3.

58. "'Goblin Market' by Christina Rossetti," *Playboy*, September 1973, p. 115.

59. Battiscombe, *A Divided Life*, pp. 106–8.

60. Ellen Golub, "Untying Goblin Apron Strings: A Psychoanalytic Reading of 'Goblin Market,'" *Literature and Psychology* 23, no. 4 (1975): 162–64.

61. A. A. De Vitis, "'Goblin Market,' Fairy Tale and Reality," *The Journal of Popular Culture* 1 (Spring 1968): 419–25.

62. Ibid., p. 425.

63. Sandra M. Gilbert and Susan Gubar, *The Madwoman in the Attic: The Woman Writer and the Nineteenth-Century Literary Imagination* (New Haven: Yale University Press, 1969), pp. 566–70.

64. Stephen Prickett, *Victorian Fantasy* (Bloomington: Indiana University Press, 1979), pp. 103–6.

65. Maureen Duffy, *The Erotic World of Faery* (London: Hodder & Stoughton, 1972), pp. 287–91.

66. Greer, "Introduction" to *Goblin Market*, p. xxxvi.

67. Ibid., p. ix.

68. C. G. Jung, "Archetypes of the Collective Unconscious," in *Twentieth Century Criticisms*, ed. William J. Handy and Max Westbrook (New York: The Free Press, 1974), pp. 206–8.

69. Conrad Festa, "Symbol and Meaning in 'A Birthday,'" *English Language Notes* 11 (September 1975): 51–56.

70. Ibid., pp. 54–55.

71. Marian Shalkhauser, "The Feminine Christ," *The Victorian Newsletter* 10 (Autumn 1956): 19–20.

72. Gilbert-Gubar, *Madwoman in the Attic*, p. 566.

73. Kaplan, "Indefinite Disclosed," p. 66.

74. Liliane Frey-Rohn, *From Freud to Jung: A Comparative Study of the Psychology of the Unconscious* (New York: G. P. Putnam's Sons for the C. G. Jung Foundation for Analytical Psychology, 1974), p. 231.

75. Ibid., p. 123.

76. Robb, *Four in Exile*, pp. 98–99.

77. Ibid., p. 99.

78. Ibid., p. 107.

79. Ibid., pp. 101–7.

80. Georgina Battiscombe, "Christina Rossetti (1830–1894)," in *British Writers: Elizabeth Gaskell and Francis Thompson,* general ed. Ian Scott-Kilver; edited under the auspices of the British Council (New York: Charles Scribner's Sons, 1982), 5:255.

81. Winston Weathers, "Christina Rossetti: The Sisterhood of Self," *Victorian Poetry* 3 (Spring 1965): 81–89.

82. Ibid., pp. 83–83.

83. Ibid., pp. 85–89.

84. Rosenblum, "Religious Poetry," pp. 48–49.

85. Hoxie Neale Fairchild, "Christina Rossetti," in *Religious Trends in English Poetry, 1830–1880,* vol. 4 of 5 vols. *Christianity and Romanticism in the Victorian Era* (New York: Columbia University Press, 1957), p. 302.

86. Robb, *Four in Exile,* p. 87.

87. Molly Mahood, *Poetry and Humanism* (Port Washington, N.Y.: Kennikat Press, 1950), p. 27.

88. Greer, "Introduction" to *Goblin Market,* pp. vii–x.

89. Zaturenska, *A Portrait with Background,* p. 242.

90. Ibid., p. 279.

91. Lucas, "Christina Rossetti," p. 137.

92. Robb, *Four in Exile,* p. 93.

93. Jerome H. Buckley, "Introduction" in *The Pre-Raphaelites* (New York: Random House, Modern Library College, 1968), p. 197.

94. Christian Murciaux, "Christina Rossetti: La Vierge Sage des Préraphaélites," *Revue de Paris,* December 1964, pp. 74–75.

95. Zaturenska *A Portrait with Background,* pp. 84–85.

96. Battiscome, Christina Rossetti, p. 21.

97. Bowra, *Romantic Imagination,* pp. 246–47.

98. Swann, *Wonder and Whimsey,* p. 23.

99. Warren Herendeen, "The Midsummer Eves of Shakespeare and Christina Rossetti," *The Victorian Newsletter* 4 (Spring 1972): 24–25.

100. Warren Herendeen, "Andrew Marvell and Christina Rossetti," *Seventeenth Century News* 20, no. 1 (Spring 1972): 9.

101. Gilbert-Gubar, *Madwoman in the Attic,* p. 574.

102. Diane D'Amico, "Christina Rossetti: The Maturin Poems," *Victorian Poetry* 19, no. 2 (Summer 1981): 130.

103. Annis Pratt, "The New Feminist Criticism," *College English* 32 (May 1971): 873.

104. Miriam Sagan, "Christina Rossetti's 'Goblin Market' and Feminist Literary Criticism, *Pre-Raphaelite Review* 3 (1980): 67.

105. Zaturenska, *A Portrait with Background,* p. 264.

106. Swan, *Wonder and Whimsey,* p. 35.

107. Ibid., p. 57.

108. Robb, *Four in Exile,* pp. 115.

109. Packer, *Christina Rossetti,* p. 330.

110. Golub, "Untying Goblin Apron Strings," p. 164.

111. Moers, *Literary Women,* p. 107.

112. Ibid., pp. 167–68.

113. Barbara Fass, "Christina Rossetti and St. Agnes' Eve," *Victorian Poetry* 14, no. 1 (Spring 1976): 35–38.

114. Ibid., p. 41.

115. Ibid., pp. 41–53.

116. Dolores Rosenblum, "Christina Rossetti: The Inward Pose," in *Shakespeare's Sisters: Feminist Essays on Women Poets*, ed. Sandra M. Gilbert and Susan Gubar (Bloomington, Indiana University Press, 1979), pp. 94–95.

117. Rosenblum, "Christina Rossetti's Religious Poetry: Watching, Looking, Keeping Vigil," pp. 36–41.

118. Gilbert-Gubar, *Madwoman in the Attic*, pp. 564–72.

119. Ibid., pp. 571–72.

120. Kaplan, "Indefinite Disclosed," pp. 64–65.

121. Ibid., pp. 69–70.

122. Gilbert-Gubar, *Madwoman in the Attic*, p. 567.

123. McGann, "Christina Rossetti's Poems," pp. 248–49.

124. Ibid., pp. 244–45.

125. Golub, "Untying Goblin Apron Strings," pp. 161–162.

126. Ibid., pp. 162–64.

127. Gisella Honnighauser, "Emblematic Tendencies in the Works of Christina Rossetti," *Victorian Poetry* 10, no. 1 (Spring 1972): 1–11.

128. De Vitis, " 'Goblin Market,' " p. 422.

129. John Adlard, "Christina Rossetti: Strategies of Loneliness," *The Contemporary Review* 221 (September 1972): 148.

130. Fass, "St. Agnes' Eve," p. 34.

131. Packer, *Christina Rossetti*, pp. 142–46.

132. Eugene J. Brzenk, " 'Up-hill and Down' by Christina Rossetti," *Victorian Poetry* 10 (1972): 368–69.

133. Robb, *Four in Exile*, p. 88.

134. Bowra, *Romantic Imagination*, p. 264.

135. Ibid., p. 266.

136. Theo Dombrowski, "Dualism in the Poetry of Christina Rossetti," *Victorian Poetry* 14, no. 1 (Spring 1976): 70–71.

137. Janowitz, "Antipodes of Self," pp. 196–98.

138. Zaturenska, *"A Portrait with Background,"* pp. 156–57.

139. Battiscombe, *Christina Rossetti*, p. 36.

140. Curran, "Lyric Voice," p. 298.

141. Ibid., p. 299.

142. Lucas, "Christina Rossetti," p. 133.

143. Lionel Stevenson, *The Pre-Raphaelite Poets* (Chapel Hill: The University of North Carolina Press, 1972, pp. 120–21.

Bibliography

Christina Rossetti's Poetical Works

Annus Dominl: A Prayer for Each Day of the Year, Founded on a Text of Holy Scripture. Edited by H. W. Burrows. London: James Parker & Co., 1874; Boston: Roberts Brothers, 1874.

Called to Be Saints: The Minor Festivals Devotionally Studied. London: Society for Promoting Christian Knowledge, 1881; New York: E. & J. B. Young, 1881.

Commonplace, and Other Short Stories. London: F. S. Ellis, 1870; Boston: Roberts Brothers, 1870.

The Complete Poems of Christina Rossetti. Vol. 1 of *Christina Georgina Rossetti, 1830–1894,* an intended three-volume Variorum edition. Edited by R. W. Crump. Baton Rouge: Louisiana State University Press, 1979.

The Face of the Deep: A Devotional Commentary on the Apocalypse. London: Society for Promoting Christian Knowledge, 1892; 3d ed., New York: E. & J. B. Young, 1895.

Goblin Market, and Other Poems with Two Designs by D. G. Rossetti. London: Macmillan, 1862; 2d ed., 1865. Reprint. Boston: Roberts Brothers, 1866.

Letter and Spirit. Notes on the Commandments. London: Society for Promoting Christian Knowledge, 1883.

Maude: A Story for Girls, with an Introduction by William Michael Rossetti. London: James Bowdon, 1896.

Monna Innominata: Sonnets and Songs by Christina G. Rossetti. Portland, Maine: T. B. Mosher, 1899.

New Poems, Hitherto Unpublished or Uncollected. Edited by William Michael Rossetti. London and New York: Macmillan, 1896.

A Pageant, and Other Poems. London and Edinburgh: Macmillan, 1881.

Poems, with Four Designs by D. G. Rossetti. New and enlarged ed. London and New York: Macmillan, 1890. Reprinted as *The Poetical Works of Christina G. Rossetti, in Two Volumes.* Boston: Litle, Brown & Co., 1902.

The Poetical Works of Christina G. Rossetti in Two Volumes. Reprint. Boston: Little Brown & Co., 1902.

The Poetical Works of Christina Georgina Rossetti. With Memoir and Notes by William Michael Rossetti. London: Macmillan, 1906.

Seek and Find. A Double Series of Short Studies of the Benedictite. London: Society for Promoting Christian Knowledge, 1869; New York: Pott, Young & Co., 1879.

Sing-Song. A Nursery Rhyme Book with 120 Illustrations by Arthur Hughes. 2d ed. London: Routledge, 1893; London and New York: Macmillan, 1893.

Speaking Likenesses with Pictures Thereof by Arthur Hughes. London: Macmillan, 1874; Boston: Roberts Brothers, 1874.

Time Flies: A Reading Diary. London: Society for Promoting Christian Knowledge, 1885.

Verses. London: Privately printed by Gaetano Polidori, 1847.

Verses, Reprinted from "Called to be Saints," "Time Flies," "The Face of the Deep." London: Society for the Promotion of Christian Knowledge, 1893. Reprint. New York: E. & J. B. Young, 1925.

The Works of General Criticism

Daiches, David. *Critical Approaches to Literature.* Englewood Cliffs, N.J.: Prentice-Hall, 1956.

de Beauvoir, Simone. *The Second Sex.* Translated and edited by H. M. Parshley. New York: Alfred A. Knopf, 1971.

Frey-Rohn, Liliane. *From Freud to Jung: A Comparative Study of the Psychology of the Unconscious.* New York: G. P. Putnam's Sons, for the C. G. Jung Foundation for Analytical Psychology, 1974.

Jung, C. G. "Archetypes of the Collective Unconscious." In *Twentieth Century Criticism,* edited by William J. Handy and Max Westbrook. New York: The Free Press, 1974.

———. *Psyche and Symbol.* New York: Doubleday Anchor Books, 1958.

Pratt, Annis. "The New Feminist Criticism." *College English* 32 (May 1971): 873–78.

Richards, I. A. *Principles of Literary Criticism.* 4th ed. London: Kegan Paul, Trench, Trubner & Co., 1930.

Ruskin, John. *Fors Clavigera in Ruskin's Works.* 4 vols. New York: Merrill & Baker, [1875] 1877.

Spacks, Patricia Ann Meyer. *The Female Imagination.* New York: Alfred A. Knopf, 1975.

Trilling, Lionel. *The Liberal Imagination: Essays on Literature and Society.* Garden City, N.Y.: Anchor Books, 1953.

The Works of Christina Rossetti's Critics

Adlard, John. "Christina Rossetti: Strategies of Loneliness." *The Contemporary Review* 221 (September 1972): 146–50.

Athenaeum, 23 June 1866, pp. 824–25.

Bald, Amelia Marjorie. *Women Writers of the Nineteenth Century.* New York: Russell & Russell, 1963.

Battiscombe, Georgina. *Christina Rossetti.* London: Longmans, Green & Co., 1965.

———. *Christina Rossetti: A Divided Life.* New York: Holt, Rinehart & Winston, 1981.

———. "Christina Rossetti (1830–1894)." *British Writers: Elizabeth Gaskell and Francis Thompson,* Vol. 5. General editor Ian Scott-Kilver. Edited under the auspices of the British Council. New York: Charles Scribner's Sons, 1982.

Bell, Mackenzie. *Christina Rossetti: A Biographical and Critical Study.* 4th ed. London: Thomas Burleigh, 1898.

Bellas, Ralph A. *Christina Rossetti.* Boston: Twayne Publishers, 1977.

Benson, Arthur Christopher. "Christina Rossetti." *The National Review* 26 (February 1895): 753–63.

Birkhead, Edith. *Christina Rossetti and Her Poetry.* London: George G. Harrap & Co., 1930.

Bowker, R. R. "London as a Literary Center." *Harper Magazine* 76 (May 1888): 815–55.

Bowra, C. M. *The Romantic Imagination.* New York: Oxford University Press, 1961.

Boyle, Sir Edward. *Biographical Essays, 1790–1890.* London: Oxford University Press, 1936. Reprint. Freeport, N.Y.: Books for Libraries Press, 1968.

Brownley, Martin Watson. "Love and Sensuality in Christina Rossetti's 'Goblin Market.'" *Essays in Literature* 6, no. 1 (Spring 1979): 179–86.

Brzenk, Eugene J. "'Up-hill and Down' by Christina Rossetti." *Victorian Poetry* 10 (1972): 367–71.

Buckley, Jerome H. Introduction to *The Pre-Raphaelites,* pp. 197–98. New York: Random House, Modern Library College, 1968.

Burdett, Osbert. *The Beardsley Period.* London: John Lany The Bodley Heat Ltd., 1925.

Caine, T. Hall. *Academy,* 27 August 1881, p. 152.

Cary, Elisabeth Luther. *The Rossettis: Dante Gabriel and Christina.* New York: G. P. Putnam's Sons, 1900.

Cazamian, Louis. *A History of English Literature: Modern Times.* Rev. ed. London: J. M. Dent & Sons, Ltd., 1927, 1930.

Chambers, Edmund K. "Review of Miss Rossetti's Verse." *Academy* 45 (February 1894): 162–64.

Charles, Edna Kotin. "A Comparative Study of Nineteenth and Twentieth Century Criticism of Selected Poems of Christina Rossetti." Ph.D. diss., New York University, 1978.

"Christina G. Rossetti." *Catholic World* 4 (March 1867): 839–46.

"Christina Georgina Rossetti." *Dial,* 16 January 1895, pp. 37–39.

"Christina Rossetti." *Saturday Review,* 5 January 1895, pp. 5–6.

"Christina Rossetti's Poems." *Catholic World* 24 (October 1876): 122–29.

Clutton-Brock, Arthur. *More Essays on Religion.* London: Methuen, 1927. Reprint. Freeport, N.Y.: Books for Libraries Press, 1971.

Coleridge, Christabel R. "The Poetry of Christina Rossetti." *Monthly Packet* 89 (March 1895): 276–82.

"Contemporary Poets and Versifiers." *Edinburgh Review* 178 (October 1893): 494–95.

Crump, R. W. *Christina Rossetti: A Reference Guide.* Boston: G. K. Hall & Co., 1976.

Cunliffe, John. *Leaders of the Victorian Revolution.* New York: D. Appleton-Century Co., 1934.

Curran, Stuart. "The Lyric Voice of Christina Rossetti." *Victorian Poetry* 9, no. 3 (Autumn 1971): 287–99.

D'Amico, Diane. Christina Rossetti: The Maturin Poems." *Victorian Poetry* 19, no. 2 (Summer 1981): 117–37.

———. "Christina Rossetti's *Later Life:* The Neglected Sonnet Sequency." *Victorian Institute Journal* 9 (1980–81): 21–28.

de Bary, Anna Bunston. "The Poetry of Christina." *Poetry Review* (London) 1 (May 1912): 203–10.

De Vitis, A. A. " 'Goblin Market' Fairy Tale and Reality." *The Journal of Popular Culture* 1 (Spring 1968): 418–26.

Dombrowski, Theo. "Dualism in the Poetry of Christina Rossetti." *Victorian Poetry* 14 no. 1 (Spring 1976): 70–76.

Duffy, Maureen. *The Erotic World of Faery.* London: Hodder & Stoughton, 1972.

Edinburgh Review 185 (October 1893): 494–95; 188 (April 1896): 514.

Elton, Oliver. *A Survey of English Literature, 1830–1880.* 2 vols. 1920. Reprint. London: Edward Arnold, Ltd., 1955.

Fairchild, Hoxie Neale. "Christina Rossetti" in *Religious Trends in English Poetry, 1830–1880.* Vol. 4, *Christianity and Romanticism in the Victorian Era,* pp. 302–16. New York: Columbia University Press, 1957.

Fass, Barbara. "Christina Rossetti and St. Agnes' Eve." *Victorian Poetry* 14, no. 1 (Spring 1976): 33–46.

Festa, Conrad. "Symbol and Meaning in 'A Birthday.' " *The English Language Notes* 11 (September 1973): 50–56.

Festa, Conrad Daniel. "Studies in Christina Rossetti's 'Goblin Market' and Other Poems." Ph.D. diss., University of South Carolina, 1969.

Foreman, Harry Baxton. "Criticism on Contemporaries. No. 6. The Rossettis. Part 1. Christina Rossetti." *Tinsley's Magazine* 5 (August 1860): 59–67.

Fredeman, William E. Review of *Christina Rossetti,* by Lona Mosk Packer. *Victorian Studies* 8 (September 1964): 71–77.

Frey-Rohn, Liliane. *From Freud to Jung: A Comparative Study of the Psychology of the Unconscious* (New York: G. P. Putnam's Sons for the C. G. Jung Foundation for Analytical Psychology, 1974).

Gilbert, Sandra M., and Gubar, Susan, eds. *The Madwoman in the Attic: The Woman Writer and the Nineteenth-Century Literary Imagination.* New Haven: Yale University Press, 1979.

———. *Shakespeare's Sisters: Feminist Essays on Women Poets.* Bloomington: Indiana University Press, 1979.

" 'Goblin Market' by Christina Rossetti." *Playboy,* September 1973, pp. 115–19.

Golub, Ellen. "Untying Goblin Apron Strings: A Psychoanalytic Reading of 'Goblin Market.' " *Literature and Psychology* 23, no. 4 (1975): 158–65.

Gosse, Sir Edmund. "Christina Rossetti." *Century Magazine* 46 (June 1893): 211–17.

Green, Eudora Zaidee. "Saint by Chance." *English Review* 62 (March 1936): 330–37.

Green, Kathleen C. "Christina Rossetti: A Study and Some Comparisons." *Cornhill Magazine* 69 (December 1930): 663–70.

Green-Armytage, A. J. *Maids of Honour.* London: Blackwood, 1906.

Greer, Germaine. "Introduction" to *Goblin Market* by Christina Rossetti, pp. vii–xxxvi. New York: Stonehill Publishing Co., 1975.

Grigson, Geoffrey. "Between Flesh and Spirit." *Times Literary Supplement*, 11 April 1980, p. 409.

Hearn, Lafcadio. "Miss Rossetti." *Complete Lectures: History of English Literature.* One-volume ed. Tokyo: Hokuseido, 1934.

Herendeen, Warren. "Andrew Marvell and Christina Rossetti." *Seventeenth Century News* 20, no. 1 (Spring 1972): 8–9.

———. "The Midsummer Eves of Shakespeare and Christina Rossetti." *Victorian Newsletter* 4 (Spring 1972): 24–26.

Honnighauser, Gisella. "Emblematic Tendencies in the Works of Christina Rossetti." *Victorian Poetry* 10, no. 1 (Spring 1972): 1–15.

Hudson, William Henry. *A Short History of English Literature in the Nineteenth Century.* London: G. Bell & Sons, 1918.

Hueffer, Ford Madox. The Collected Poems of Christina Rossetti." *Fortnightly Review* 75 (March 1904): 393–405.

———. "Christina Rossetti and Pre-Raphaelite Love." In *Memories and Impressions: A Study in Atmospheres.* New York: Harper, 1911.

Hunt, Violet. *The Wife of Rossetti.* New York: E. P. Dutton & Co., 1932.

Janowitz, K. E. "The Antipodes of Self: Three Poems by Christina Rossetti." *Victorian Poetry* 11, no. 3 (14 December 1973); pp 195–205.

Johnson, Lionel. "Literature: Miss Rossetti and Mrs. Alexander." *Academy*, 25 July 1896, pp. 59–60.

Kaplan, Cora. "The Indefinite Disclosed: Christina Rossetti and Emily Dickinson." In *Women Writing and Writing about Women.* Edited by Mary Jacobus. New York: Barnes & Noble Books, 1979.

Kent, Muriel. "Christina Rossetti: A Reconsideration." *Contemporary Review* 138 (December 1930): 759–67.

Kenyon, James Benjamin. "Dante Gabriel Rossetti and His Sister Christina." *Methodist Review* 78 (September 1896): 743–53.

Law, Alice. "The Poetry of Christina G. Rossetti." *Westminster Review* 143 (April 1895): 444–53.

Le Gallienne, Richard. "Christina Rossetti." *Academy*, 7 February 1891, pp. 130–31.

Levy, Amy. "The Poetry of Christina Rossetti." *Woman's World* (London) 1 (February 1888): 178–80.

Literary World (Boston) 6 (May 1876): 181–82.

Literature, 22 January 1898, pp. 66–68.

London Quarterly Review 87 (October 1896): 2–16.

Lowther, George. "Christina Rossetti." *Contemporary Review* 104 (November 1913): 681–89.

Lucas, F. L. "Christina Rossetti." *Ten Victorian Poets.* 3d ed. Cambridge, England, University Press, 1940.

McGann, Jerome J. "Christina Rossetti's Poems: A New Edition and a Revaluation." *Victorian Studies* 23 (Winter 1980): 237–58.

Mackenzie, Margaret. "Fettered Christina Rossetti." *Thought: Fordham University Quarterly* 7 (January 1932): 32–43.

Madeleva, Sister M. *Chaucer's Nuns and Other Essays.* Port Washington, N.Y.: Kennikat Press, 1925.

Mahood, Molly. *Poetry and Humanism.* Port Washington, N.Y.: Kennikat Press, Inc., 1950.

Mason, Eugene. *A Book of Preferences in Literature.* New York: E. P. Dutton, 1915.

Mather, Frank Jewett, Jr. "The Rossettis." *Bookman* (New York) 39 (April 1919): 137–47.

Meynell, Alice. "Christina Rossetti." *New Review* 12 (February 1895): 201–6.

"Miss Rossetti's New Poems." *Athenaeum,* 10 September 1881, pp. 327–28.

"Miss Rossetti's Poems." *Saturday Review* 81 (February 1896): 194–97.

Moers, Ellen. *Literary Women.* Garden City, N.Y.: Doubleday, 1976.

Moore, Virginia. "Letters and Comments: Christina Rossetti's Centennial." *Yale Review* 20 (December 1930): 428–32.

More, Paul Elmer. "Christina Rossetti." *Atlantic Monthly* 94 (December 1904): 815–21.

Morse-Boycott, Desmond Lionel. "Christina Rossetti, 1830–1894." *Lead, Kindly Light: Studies of the Saints and Heroes of the Oxford Movement.* New York: Macmillan, 1933.

Murciaux, Christian. "Christina Rossetti: La Vierge Sage des Préraphaélites." *Revue de Paris,* December 1964, pp. 74–84.

[Nicholl, W. Robertson]. "Mr. Bell's 'Christina Rossetti.' " *Bookman* (London) 13 (February 1898): 154.

Norton, Mrs. Charles Eliot. " 'The Angel in the House' and 'The Goblin Market.' " *Macmillan's Magazine,* 7 September 1863, p. 404.

Osmond, Percy H. *The Mystical Poets of the English Church.* London: Society for the Promotion of Christian Knowledge, 1919.

Packer, Lona Mosk. *Christina Rossetti.* Berkeley: University of California Press, 1963.

Payne, W. M. *Dial,* 6 April 1896, pp. 205–6.

"Poems by Mr. and Mrs. Rossetti." *Ecclesiastic and Theologian* 24 (September 1962): 419–29.

Prickett, Stephen. *Victorian Fantasy.* Bloomington: Indiana University Press, 1979.

Raleigh, Sir Walter. *Letters of Sir Walter Raleigh.* Edited by Lady Raleigh. 2 vols. London: Methuen & Co., 1926.

Reilly, Joseph L. "Christina Rossetti." *America: A Catholic Review of the Week,* 14 February 1931, pp. 460–61.

———. *Dear Prue's Husband and Other People.* New York: Macmillan, 1932.

Robb, Nesca A. "Christina Rossetti." *Four in Exile.* London: Hutchinson, 1948.

Rosenblum, Dolores. "Christina Rossetti: The Inward Pose." In *Shakespeare's Sisters: Feminist Essays on Women Poets,* edited by Sandra M. Gilbert and Susan Gubar. Bloomington: Indiana University Press, 1979.

———. "Christina Rossetti's Religious Poetry: Watching, Looking, Keeping Vigil." *Victorian Poetry* 20, no. 1 (Spring 1982): 33–49.

"Rossetti, Christina Georgina." *Dictionary of National Biography,* 17:282–84. New York: Macmillan, 1897.

Rossetti, Geoffrey W. "Christina Rossetti." *Criterion* 10 (October 1930): 95–117.

Rossetti, William Michael. *Preraphaelite Diaries and Letters.* London: Hurst & Blackett, 1900.

———. *Some Reminiscences.* 2 vols. London: Brown Langham, 1906.

———, ed. *Dante Gabriel Rossetti: His Family Letters, with a Memoir.* 2 vols. Boston: Roberts Brothers, 1895.

———, ed. "Memoir and Notes." In *The Poetical Works of Christina Georgina Rossetti.* London: Macmillan, 1904.

"The Rossettis." *Literary World,* 5 November 1881, pp. 395–96.

[Rudd, F. A.]. "Christina Rossetti." *Catholic World* 4 (March 1867): 839–46.

Sagan, Miriam. "Christina Rossetti's 'Goblin Market' and Feminist Literary Criticism." *Pre-Raphaelite Review* 3 (1980): 66–74.

Saintsbury, George. *Historical Manual of English Prosody from the Twelfth Century to the Present Day.* Vol. 3. London: Macmillan, 1910.

Sanders, Mary Frances. *The Life of Christina Rossetti.* London: Hutchinson Co. (Publishers) Ltd., 1930.

Sawtell, Margaret. *Christina Rossetti: Her Life and Religion.* London: A. R. Mobray & Co., 1955.

Scott, William Bell. *Autobiographical Notes of the Life of William Bell Scott, and Notices of His Artistic and Poetic Circle of Friends, 1839–1882.* London: Harper & Brothers, 1892.

Shalkhauser, Marian. "The Feminine Christ." *Victorian Newsletter* 10 (Autumn 1956): 19–20.

Shove, Fredegond. *Christina Rossetti: A Study.* 1931. Reprint. New York: Octagon Press, 1969.

Smellie, A. "Christina Rossetti and Her Message." *Wesleyan Methodist Magazine* 118 (1895): 203–6.

"Some Women Poets." *Living Age,* 1 April 1899, pp. 26–34.

Sontag, Susan. *Against Interpretation and Other Essays.* New York: Farrar, Straus & Giroux, 1966.

Stevenson, Lionel. *The Pre-Raphaelite Poets.* Chapel Hill: The University of North Carolina Press, 1972.

Stuart, Dorothy Margaret. *Christina Rossetti.* London: Macmillan, 1930.

Swann, Thomas Barnett. *Wonder and Whimsy.* Francetown, N.J.; Marshall Jones Co., 1960.

[Symons, Arthur]. "Miss Rossetti's Poetry." *London Quarterly Review* 88 (July 1887): 338–50.

Taylor, Bayard. "Christina Rossetti." *Critical Essays and Literary Notes.* New York: Putnam's Sons, 1880.

Thomas, Edward. *The Last Sheaf: Essays.* Frome, Great Britain: Butler & Tanner Ltd., 1928.

Thomas, Eleanor Walter. *Christina Georgina Rossetti.* 1931. Reprint. New York: AMS Press, 1966.

Thompson, Alexander Hamilton. "Christina Rossetti." *Cambridge History of English Literature.* Vol. 13, part 2. New York: Macmillan, 1917.

Tuell, Anne Kimball. "Christina Rossetti." In *A Victorian at Bay.* Boston: Marshall, Jones, 1932.

"Victorian Romantics." *Times Literary Supplement,* 14 November 1929, p. 919.

Walker, Hugh, and Walker, Mrs. Hugh. *Outlines of Victorian Literature.* Cambridge, England: University Press, 1919.

Watson, Lily. "Christina Rossetti." *Sunday at Home,* 5 May 1894, pp. 425–28.

Weideman, Rebecca Sue. "A Critical Bibliography of Christina Rossetti." Ph.D. diss., University of Texas at Austin, 1979.

Watts-Dutton, Theodore. "Christina Georgina Rossetti." *Athenaeum,* 15 January 1896, pp. 207–9.

Waugh, Arthur. *Reticence in Literature.* London: J. G. Wilson, 1915.

Weathers, Winston. "Christina Rossetti: The Sisterhood of Self." *Victorian Poetry* 3 (Spring 1965): 81–89.

Williamson, Claude C. H. "A Few Lines on Christina Rossetti." *Writers of Three Centuries, 1789–1914.* Philadelphia: George W. Jacobs & Co., Publishers, 1915.

Winwar, Francis [Frances Grebanier, pseud.]. *Poor Splendid Wings: The Rossettis and Their Circle.* Boston: Little, Brown, 1933.

Woolf, Virginia. *The Second Common Reader.* New York: Harcourt, Brace & Co., 1932.

Zabel, Morton Dauwen. "Christina Rossetti and Emily Dickinson." *Poetry* 37 (January 1931): 213–16.

Zaturenska, Marya. *Christina Rossetti: A Portrait with Background.* New York: Macmillan, 1949.

Index

World, The, 24
Wrestling, 109
Wylie, Elinor, 97

Yale Review, 71, 75, 97–98

Year's Windfall, A, 54

Zabel, Morton Dauwen, 97
Zaturenska, Marya, 111–12, 120–21, 138, 141, 156